THE STUDENTS LIBRARY OF EDUCATION has been designed to meet the needs of students of Education at Colleges of Education and at University Institutes and Departments. It will also be valuable for practising teachers and educationists. The series takes full account of the latest developments in teacher-training and of new methods and approaches in education. Separate volumes will provide authoritative and up-to-date accounts of the topics within the major fields of sociology, philosophy and history of education, educational psychology, and method. Care has been taken that specialist topics are treated lucidly and usefully for the non-specialist reader. Altogether, the Students Library of Education will provide a comprehensive introduction and guide to anyone concerned with the study of education, and with educational theory and practice.

This is an unusual and ambitious type of introduction to educational theory. Mr Moore is interested in and has respect for some of the thinkers of the past such as Plato, Rousseau, James Mill and Dewey whose works tend to be neglected nowadays. But his interest in them is not a purely historical one. Although he is critical of them at various points he thinks that they provide useful examples of educational theory from which much can be learnt.

Mr Moore resists strongly the suggestion that educational theory should be assimilated to or judged on criteria appropriate to scientific theory. He sees it rather as a complex structure of different types of assumptions bound together by the relevance of all of them to educational practice. It contains scientific assumptions, for instance, about human nature and learning. But these have to be placed in a context provided by value judgments about aims and philosophical assumptions about the nature of knowledge. Mr Moore examines the ways in which thinkers of the past have

v

tried to knit together these different types of assumptions and suggests lines along which a modern theory can be developed which is both logically respectable and relevant to present day needs.

The value of Mr Moore's introduction lies not just in the clarity and brevity with which he deals with difficult issues which any serious student of education must understand. It lies also in his attempt to link the old approach to the study of education via the Great Educators with the modern problem-centred approach.

R. S. PETERS

Contents

CONTENTS

Acknowledgments

This book owes much to Professor P. H. Hirst and Professor D. J. O'Connor whose writings on educational theory clarified my own thoughts on this topic and gave them direction. My intellectual debt to Professor R. S. Peters will be obvious throughout the book, but it gives me great pleasure to acknowledge it here. Professor Peters increased my obligations to him by reading the work in draft and saving me from many errors.

Jim Burch and Robert Dearden discussed an early draft with me and I profited greatly by their criticisms. Denis Lawton and Fitz Taylor helped me with Chapter 5. Frances Mawer produced the typescript most efficiently. I am grateful to these colleagues for their help. I accept full responsibility for the errors and shortcomings which remain.

I

Educational theory

i Introduction

Educational theory has seldom been a popular subject, with teachers in training or with established teachers. It is not difficult to find reasons for this. There persists a conviction that educational theory is unnecessary. It is often thought that all the would-be teacher requires is a knowledge of his subjects and a confident manner. Academic knowledge can be won by study; the confident manner can be assumed. Pedagogical skill can be acquired, if at all, in the classroom, by watching more experienced teachers work and by using one's common sense. Nothing more is needed. So when training colleges insist on some theoretical work in education as well as practical training this is often seen as an unrewarding addition to the student's burden.

Another reason for its unpopularity is that, until quite recently, student teachers were usually required to study, under the heading of educational theory, historical accounts of the work of the 'great educators', often with little guidance as to the contemporary relevance or practical value of this study. This led students to ask what it all had to do with their immediate problems, with the schools they had to teach in and the children they had to teach. Plato and Comenius seemed to have little to say on these matters. Questions like these are easier to ask than to answer, as college lecturers soon discover, and these pertinent questions were not always satisfactorily answered. Consequently a general uneasiness about the whole subject has grown up. The elementary psychology which was included in it could usually be shown to have some relevance to teaching, but this apart, educational theory always seemed to be on the defensive and in need of apologetic justification. Not surprisingly it has usually been studied, and sometimes taught, with some indifference, and tends nowadays to be written off as out-of-date, or irrelevant.

Practising teachers as a rule have little enthusiasm for it. They often remember it as an uncongenial college subject, and if they meet it again in their professional work they may regard it as something which has been wished on them by 'experts' remote from their workaday classrooms and having to do with proposals which may conflict with well-tried ways. So it is often dismissed by them as 'mere theory', as opposed to common sense practice.

Quite apart from this teacherly lack of enthusiasm, there have been in recent years reservations about its academic integrity. It has been suggested that educational theory, especially as it has been traditionally understood, is something of a fraud, that there really is no such thing as *educational* theory. What collects under this heading, it is alleged, is often very little more than the pronouncements of the more imaginative of those who have been concerned with practical pedagogy, mixed up with some psychology and sociology and some philosophising of a vague and uplifting sort, but having no underlying discipline or unity of structure. Educational theory is contrasted with scientific theory and it is observed that whereas scientists formulate theories which can be shown to be valid or invalid by publicly-agreed procedures, this is not the case with those who offer so-called theories of education. There are, it is suggested, no such procedures for showing an educational theory as such to be sound or unsound. At most, scientific stringency applies only to that part of it which comes under the heading of psychology and sociology, but educational theory usually contains a good deal more than this. The implication here is that in an educational theory, apart from the psychology and sociology contained in it, almost anything can be said, since this extra material is not likely to be amenable to any rigorous checking. (7, Ch. 2)* So, it is claimed, such theories are not really theories at all. The term 'educational theory' should be used to refer only to those parts of psychology and sociology which have a bearing on educational practice; any other use of the term is a misnomer. (28, Ch. 5)

Educational theory, then, is generally under attack. This book tries to come to its defence. The enterprise will be conducted in three stages. In Chapters 1 and 2 there will be an attempt to restore educational theory to academic respectability. It will be maintained that educational theory *is* theory and that an educational theory, taken as a whole, may be open to criticism of a sufficiently stringent kind as to warrant its status as a candidate for confirmation or reasoned rejection. It will be suggested that it is not the case that

* Number references in the text refer to the bibliography on pages 100-2.

in an educational theory as such anything can be said. The point will be made, however, that it is educational theory which is at issue and not something else, and that educational theory should be judged for what it is and not as though it were a fraudulent version of another kind of theory. In Chapters 3 and 4 some of the more influential theories of education of the past will be outlined and discussed. The case will be put that these theories, however imperfect, do qualify as theories and that despite their shortcomings they have something to offer to teachers which is not irrelevant, impractical or even, in important respects, out of date. Finally, in Chapters 5 and 6 it will be argued that a grasp of educational theory is an important part of a teacher's professional equipment and suggestions offered about the way in which an adequate on-going theory might be developed.

ii Theory

To understand the nature of educational theory we must be clear about what, in general, a theory is. This is a complicated matter and we shall try so far as possible to simplify it rather than dwell on its complexities. In everyday talk we may use the word 'theory' to cover a number of different though related situations. We might say, 'I have a theory that . . .' and mean that we can give a tentative explanation of some puzzling state of affairs. A householder might say he has a theory that the condensation on the living-room wall was caused by the room being too cold. A passenger waiting on a railway station might put forward the theory that it was fog which was making the train late. Sherlock Holmes, in the story called 'The Speckled Band', formed a theory that the lady died because someone pushed a poisonous snake through the ventilator, on top of her, during the night. In each case, 'theory' refers to an attempt to explain how things have come to be as they are—the damp walls, the late train, the victim. The word is also used to cover attempts to explain what is likely to happen in the future. In the eighteenth century, Thomas Malthus formed a theory that population tended to increase more rapidly than food supplies, and that certain social consequences would follow if the two rates were not brought artificially into line. Here the theory was, at least partly, predictive; an attempt to explain what might be expected to occur.

In a different though related sense we may speak of 'theory' as a contrast to 'practice'. The apprentice plumber thinks of 'theory' as what he does at evening classes, as distinct from what he does during his working day. He does his 'theory' on paper, whereas his 'practice' involves the use of materials and tools. Similarly we could talk about the theory of foreign exchanges, as contrasted with what

3

financial operators do in their offices. In these cases, too, 'theory' could be said to cover explanations of how things come to be as they are, in the world of plumbing or finance, and also of what might be expected in the future.

What links up all these examples is that there is in each case a reference to a body of knowledge or belief. The householder has some knowledge about the effects of temperature on humidity; the railway passenger knows that fog often holds up trains. Sherlock Holmes had a belief about the motives and methods of Dr Roylott. The apprentice plumber, doing his 'theory', acquires knowledge which explains the functioning of cisterns and pipes. Malthus based his predictions on his beliefs about the growth of population and food supplies. The financial expert knows about the movement of currency rates. In each case this body of knowledge or belief is the basis of an attempt to explain some state of affairs, past, present or future. Here then we have one important aspect of the nature of theory: its role as explaining, on the basis of some assumed belief, what happens, has happened, or is likely to happen. This aspect points to the central or paradigm sense of the term 'theory', that is, an instrument for reasoned explanation and prediction. We find 'theory' used like this in what is comprehensively called 'science'. Science is an activity which tries to explain in general terms what happens in the world of phenomena. People tend to think of 'theory' as being primarily connected with activity of this kind, hence the popular view that the 'proper' sense of theory is 'scientific' theory.

We may now set out some characteristic features of a scientific theory so that we can compare educational theory with it. Scientific theory, we said, is an attempt to give a general explanation of something that goes on in the world. What we loosely call 'the world' is a complicated network of things, events and situations. These elements tend to occur in patterns. There are discernible uniformities in our experience. The scientist is interested in these uniformities. His task is to make sense of our world by taking account of them. He tries to establish the existence of such uniformities where they are not obvious and to plot the connections between one set of uniformities and another. In this way he can explain what happens and predict the future course of events. Strictly we ought here to make a distinction between a scientific 'hypothesis' and a 'theory'. A 'hypothesis', in the scientific sense, is a statement of some supposed uniformity in nature: that gases expand when they are heated, or that unsupported material objects fall towards the earth. A hypothesis, when established, becomes a 'law of nature', a general statement of uniformity observed in nature. The term 'theory' in its strict scientific sense is perhaps best understood as an attempt to account for a number of hypotheses

4

or laws of nature by bringing them under a more general explanation still. An example of this was Newton's attempt to explain the movements of matter by saying, in effect, that every instance of such a movement might be brought under a general law that objects attract each other according to their relative mass and in some proportion to the distance between them. This 'theory' helps to explain such different phenomena as the falling of the rain, the incidence of tides and the orbits of planets, by bringing several separate explanations under one more comprehensive law. Another example is the work of the geophysicist Wegener who was struck by various continuities in the rock structures of different land masses and tried to explain these coincidences by suggesting that there had been a drift of continents from a central land-mass. Newton's theory of gravity, Wegener's theory of continental drift, Darwin's theory of natural selection are all examples of this higher-order explanation of established uniformities. (1, Ch. 12)

Now, although this distinction between hypothesis and theory can be made, the term 'theory' is often used, even in popular scientific writing, in a less strict way than this, and the two terms are often used synonymously. Since this book is about educational theory rather than scientific theory we shall not complicate our account by insisting on this distinction, and we shall, when talking about the scientist, follow the less strict form, and use the term 'theory' to cover both hypotheses which may amount to laws of nature and those higher-order theories which try to fit together generalisations into still more general laws. Little turns on this point so far as we are concerned.

It is important for a scientific theory that it should square with the known facts, that the explanation it offers should be a correct one. The scientist, when he is trying to establish his theory, looks for evidence available to him in the empirical world. This will involve him in systematic observation and experiment. If the theory is found not to fit all the known facts it has to be amended or discarded. If it does account for and explain the relevant facts it is taken as confirmed and it becomes part of the wider body of natural laws.

iii   Explanatory theories and practical theories

If we look at educational theory in the writings of the 'great educators' of the past, we find that it does not agree very closely with the account of scientific theory given above. Plato, Rousseau, Froebel and the others did not, in their educational theorising, go about their task in the way that a scientist would go about his. Their theories contain very little reference to observations or experiments of a systematic kind, about children, for example, and the way they develop, or about teaching methods and their effectiveness. What we usually find is that the writer begins with certain assumptions about what can be done or ought to be done in education, and on the basis of these assumptions makes some recommendations about what teachers and others should do. Not all these assumptions are of the kind which would be amenable to scientific investigation, but even in the case of those that are, we do not generally find that these writers try to arrive at them as a scientist would try to do. Assumptions about the nature of children, for example, are often adopted unargued, or derived from other assumptions not themselves established empirically. Nor are the conclusions arrived at in the theories such as can be checked against the facts of the world, as the conclusions of a scientific theory would be. It is because of this that Plato, Froebel and Rousseau have been accused of not really being educational *theorists* at all. Their pronouncements and recommendations, it is alleged, are not the kind which can be tested by reference to the observable world, nor are they always based on evidence which can be checked in this way. There is some truth in this, but rather more needs to be said. It is one thing to show that educational theorists in the past have made assumptions and pronouncements which are not empirically testable, but quite another to conclude that educational theory as such is not theory at all. The shortcomings of the traditional theorists certainly tell against their particular theories, but the question still remains whether educational theory itself can be defended against the charge that it is not really theory at all, or theory only by courtesy. This charge now needs to be examined.

It is important to recognise a difference between scientific theories, and another class of theories, amongst which we will include theories of education. Science is fundamentally a matter of explanation. The main point of doing science is to learn the truth about the world and to express this truth as laws of nature. It is true that such laws, once established, can be used not only to explain what happens, but also to enable us to predict and to some extent to control the future. But it is not the scientist's job as such to recommend what use shall be made of the knowledge he makes available. How we can control future events may be a scientific matter, but the decision to exercise this control, and the particular form it should take, is not. Malthus may have been giving a scientific theory when he maintained that population tends to outstrip food supplies and that the balance is naturally restored by famine and disease; but when he used the theory as the basis for counselling against early marriages or poor-relief, he was not doing science but something else. He was offering practical advice to administrators and others. Thus we can make a distinction between explanatory theories, like those of Newton and Wegener, and *practical* theories. We shall deal with the details of practical theories later on. Here we may note that the scientist's job, as scientist, is not primarily practical but explanatory. His job is to find out. Education, however, is primarily a *practical* enterprise. What sort of practical enterprise it is needs to be looked into more closely, but essentially it involves getting something done, changing the attitudes and behaviour of people, usually those of children. The task of the educationalist, the teacher, is to get something done in the world.

This distinction is important. For whilst scientific theory is basically descriptive and explanatory, educational theory, it can be argued, does not set out to explain what the world is like. Rather, as P. H. Hirst has maintained, its primary function is to guide educational practice. (20) (22) Its function is primarily *prescriptive* or recommendatory. The difference may be put simply by saying that whereas scientific theory tries to tell us what is the case, educational theory, like theories in morals, medicine and politics, tries to tell us what we should do. This does not mean that in some circumstances educational theory could not be used to explain what is happening, in, say, a lesson, but education is primarily practical in function, and educational theory is primarily practical theory. We can perhaps now see that one possible objection to educational theory, that it doesn't operate in all respects like scientific theory, is misplaced. It isn't a valid objection to educational theory that its conclusions can't be, in all respects, checked against the facts of the empirical world, since educational theories do not try to give an explanation of the way the world is. Educational theory doesn't operate like scientific theory, and isn't altogether amenable to the tests of scientific method. This doesn't mean that we have saved educational theory from all the objections which might be raised against it. There remains the problem of how its pronouncements are to be validated. The point is, however, that educational theory is not to be denied the title of theory simply because it doesn't conform in all respects to a scientific theory. The fact that the word 'theory' is most commonly understood in a scientific context doesn't mean that when it is used in other senses it is used wrongly or misleadingly. It would be wrong to suppose that the only reliable or authentic theories are scientific theories. This would be like supposing that chess wasn't really a game because no ball is used, or that 'Patience' isn't a proper game because the player has no opponent. Games are no less games because they are played on boards or without a ball or by oneself. (43, s. 66) And, as there are different kinds of activities called games, so there are different kinds of theories. Scientific theory, descriptive and explanatory, is one kind; practical theories, where the point is not explanation but prescription, are another. The fact that these predominantly practical theories are not 'scientific' in the central sense, does not warrant their being excluded as theories. Nor are they inferior sorts of theories. They are theories of a different kind.

iv Educational theory and philosophy of education

We can now give a preliminary picture of the nature and role of an educational theory. To do this we make use of what might be called a 'model', a device which enables us to comprehend a complicated situation by seeing it in simplified terms. Let us think of education as involving an interrelated set of activities going on at different levels, something like a building with more than one floor occupied. On the ground floor there go on various 'educational activities'—teaching, learning, training, demonstrating, punishing—the sort of activities to be found in classrooms anywhere. At the next higher level, say at the first-floor level, there is educational theory, which may be understood as a body of connected principles, counsels and recommendations, aimed at influencing what goes on at the ground-floor level. At a higher level still there is philosophy of education, which has for its main tasks the clarification of the concepts used at lower levels, concepts like 'educating' and 'teaching' for example, and an examination of theories which operate there, testing them for consistency and validity. The differences in level are to be understood as 'logical' differences, which means, roughly, that each higher stage arises out of, and depends on, the stage below. Educational theory, for example, presupposes educational activities and depends upon them for its point. Philosophy of education presupposes both educational activities and educational theories. Educational theorising, like philosophy of education, may be called a higher-order activity, since it operates on related activities which go on at a lower logical level. Educational theory, then, is a higher-order enterprise, a practical theory which aims at guiding those engaged in educational activities, in schools and elsewhere. The great writers in educational theory, Plato, Locke, Rousseau, Mill and Dewey, for example, may be thought of as each giving a more or less worked-out body of prescriptions for the guidance of teachers. This last statement gives perhaps an oversimplified account and to correct it we must anticipate a point made in a later chapter. We may say that the theories offered by these writers are 'general' theories of education, theories which try to give comprehensive, over-arching guidance in the conduct of education, and which are usually associated with a distinctive social and political position. One further point needs to be noticed here. The term 'educational theory' is sometimes used to cover writing of various kinds *about* education, so that what are really psychological, sociological and philosophical discussions of educational issues may be included under this broad heading. An objection to this practice is that it makes the notion of 'educational theory' unwieldy and confusing, since much theorising *about* education doesn't amount to giving a theory *of* education. In this book 'educational theory' will be understood in the narrower sense indicated here to refer to an organised body of principles and recommendations directed towards those concerned with educational practice. Educational theory will be theory *of* education.

v *Psychology and sociology*

So far we have tried to absolve educational theory from the charge that it isn't really theory at all. We have tried to do this by arguing that the role of educational theory is different from that of scientific theory, and that the standard for judging scientific theories is not in all respects appropriate for judging the validity of educational theories. What has not yet been done is to show that an educational theory is capable of being validated in its own way. This will be dealt with more fully in the next chapter. As a move towards this, however, it can be shown that, despite the difference between the two types of theory there is none the less a close connection between them. If a practical theory is to be validated at all its conclusions must not run counter to any established scientific truths. Practical conclusions must be empirically possible. So, within the framework of a general practical theory, a general theory of education, let us say, there is a place for theories of the scientific kind. These theories will contribute to the practical theory by providing the empirical knowledge required as a realistic basis for what is recommended.

To make this point clearer we may look briefly at the ways in which the two sciences most closely connected with education, psychology and sociology, can contribute to educational theory. Some actual contributions from these sciences will be discussed later on in this book. Only the general nature of their contributions need be mentioned here.

The psychologist and the sociologist may contribute to educational theory in two important ways. To illustrate this we may recur to a point made earlier and distinguish between theories *about* education and theories of education. Theories *about* education take

9

education as a datum and make generalisations about it, trying to explain its function in terms of, say, social or individual needs, or tracing its origins, its history or its social influence. Thus there could be psychological and sociological theories about education as well as historical or political theories about it. A psychologist, for example, might advance the theory that education helps people to integrate more adequately into social life or that it increases mental stability or possibly that it creates nervous tension unknown in a primitive society. A sociologist might maintain that changes in the content of education follow rather than initiate social change, or that a common public education increases social solidarity. Whether these suggestions are true or not is immaterial here. The point is that they would be theories *about* education, and showing them to be true or false would involve carrying out investigations of a straightforwardly scientific kind.

The psychologist and the sociologist can also contribute to theories *of* education, theories which involve a body of prescriptions to guide practice. They can contribute by providing empirical evidence upon which rules of practice may be rationally grounded. The psychologist may discover facts about the ways in which children develop and how they acquire the conceptual apparatus they need to make sense of their world. He may be able to give reliable information about the conditions under which learning takes place, and how individuals may be motivated to learn. He may be able to tell us what effects different regimes of child-nurture and child-management will have on children's development and their behaviour in school. Similarly the sociologist may be able to give information about the influence of different social factors on the child's attitudes towards school and on his ability and desire to learn, what the effect of different parental attitudes towards education will be, and what effects differences in social class will have on the child's educational progress. Here too, the results of his work will be the contribution of a scientist to the theory *of* education, information of the empirical kind without which no sound educational practice is likely. The findings of the psychologist and the sociologist would thus themselves be theories *within* educational theory, explanations operating as the empirical basis for the recommendations made. To perform this function adequately these contributory theories must themselves be well-grounded as scientific theories. The important educational theories of the past usually included what would now be called psychological and sociological assumptions as the basis of their recommendations. Unfortunately these supposedly factual assumptions were sometimes dubious and untestable and sometimes false. Just how far this was so we may discover when we examine some of these theories. But the fact that some of the assumptions written in to educational theories lack scientific validity in no way shows that educational theory as such is invalid or fails to qualify as theory. That an educational theory of the over-arching kind bases its recommendations on doubtful or erroneous grounds would be a reason for rejecting it but, as will be maintained later on, there is no good reason why an educational theory should not make full use of the factual findings of psychologists, sociologists and others and thus be, so far as this aspect of the theory is concerned, as scientifically respectable as could be wished.

vi Conclusion

This chapter has tried to do two things. First, to distinguish between two types of theories, explanatory and practical, and to put scientific theories into one category and theories of education into the other. The point of this was to suggest that we should not dismiss educational theory as theory simply because it isn't scientific theory. Second, to show that although the two kinds of theory are different there is, none the less, a connection between them. Educational theory, we shall find, contains elements not found in strictly scientific theories, and so its validation or rejection is not simply a matter of squaring its conclusions with empirical findings. It is, however, true that if practical recommendations to teachers are to be acceptable they must be grounded on a correct understanding of what the world is like, and especially that part of the world constituted by the nature of children, their development, the way they learn and the way they react to social influences. So there will inevitably be a scientific component in any adequate theory of education. A valid scientific theory gives an adequate explanation of what happens in the world, based on established evidence: a valid educational theory would be one which gave adequate recommendations for practice, once again based on adequate and appropriate evidence. An objection to many of the educational theorists of the past is that the supposedly factual assumptions they adopted as the basis of their prescriptions, assumptions which should have been scientifically grounded, were not always so. They were often content to use unargued or untestable assumptions where scientific knowledge was required. This was sometimes inevitable since the relevant scientific knowledge was not available to them, but in so far as their theories lacked this scientific grounding they were open to criticism, however perceptive the writers were and however valuable in other ways their insights may have been.

2

The structure of educational theory

i *Limited and general theories*

In this chapter we examine the formal structure of an educational theory, and discuss how such a theory might be validated. To begin with we may make a distinction between 'limited' and 'general' theories of education.

Limited theories of education involve prescriptions of a mainly pedagogical kind, about the most effective ways of teaching. An example would be that whatever is taught should be linked up with some experience of the pupil so that he can make sense of the new material. Another is the injunction to teachers to 'proceed from the concrete to the abstract', from facts to principles. Both of these would be pedagogical theories in that they involve recommendations for successful teaching; both would be limited to this technical purpose. Such theories need not be put explicitly in the form of a recommendation. Those quoted above could just as easily have been given as: 'Pupils tend to learn most effectively if their work is linked with their previous experience, or if they proceed from present concrete experience of things to abstraction and generalisation.' A recommendation for practice may be implied in what is on the face of it a factual assertion. For example, an important educational theory of this limited kind is that the nature of a subject to a large extent determines how it must be taught. In mathematics, for instance, the grasp of some points presupposes knowledge and understanding of others. We can't really understand what is involved in the notion of 'triangle' until we have grasped the notion of 'angle', and 'angle' can only be understood when we understand what is meant by a 'line'. The theory is thus given in terms of the logical dependence of one concept upon another, but implicit in this is the recommendation that we should teach in a certain way—according to the 'logical order' of the material. There will be an indefinite number of such limited theories, giving recommendations about teaching techniques, the ways of motivating children, of getting their interest and of keeping them in order. They will be part of the professional equipment of the teacher. It is new or unfamiliar theories of this limited kind which may get an unsympathetic reception from practising teachers, especially if they are thought to come from 'experts' from behind the educational lines.

In saying that they are educational theories, making or implying practical recommendations to teachers, we are of course saying that they have a general application. They are meant to guide teachers generally. They are none the less limited in that they do not themselves involve any comprehensive notion of what 'education' is or what its purpose is. Their connection with education is only contingent since they could be effective in situations where we might hesitate to say that 'education' was going on at all. Education in at least one of its senses involves more than teaching, more even than successful teaching. In so far as they are connected with education, they are merely part of its mechanism and as limited, pedagogical theories they would normally take place in a more general, 'over-arching' theory of education. General theories of education are more far-reaching in their scope and purpose. They include not simply recommendations about the conditions of effective teaching but recommendations for producing a certain type of person, sometimes even a certain type of society. The theories of education of Plato, Rousseau, James Mill and Dewey are general theories. These writers certainly offer pedagogical prescriptions, but they do much more than this. They are concerned with the making of an educated man, and their recommendations cover not only what they consider to be the best ways of teaching but also what is to be taught and to what end. It is with such general theories of education that we shall be concerned in this book.

ii *Structure of scientific theory*

General theories of education will differ from each other quite considerably, according to what each aims at producing by way of an 'educated man', but they all have certain features in common. One already mentioned is that they are all primarily practical or prescriptive in character, giving overall recommendations about what ought to be done. To bring out clearly what other features they share we need to examine the *structure* of a practical theory, to see what such a theory involves.

It will be useful to compare this structure with that of a general theory of the scientific kind, a general explanatory theory. The methodology of science is complicated and controversial and it is not intended to enter into this subject any further than is needed for a brief comparison. A major controversy in the philosophy of science has centred on the way in which scientific hypotheses or theories are arrived at and established as valid. One version is that a scientific theory emerges from the observation of a large number of particular instances of a phenomenon, each of which is found to have, let us say, a certain characteristic. It is noted that, for example, every case of a ray of light passing through a glass prism is also a case of the light being deflected at a certain angle. Or, it is observed that whenever a gas is heated it expands in volume. So, by observation and experiment, a connection is established between one phenomenon and another, and this connection may be expressed as: All cases of P are also cases of Q. Where the number of positive instances is very large and there have been no counter-instances the generalisation is established as a well-grounded hypothesis, a law of nature, and is held to apply not only to the instances actually observed but also to those as yet unobserved and perhaps unobservable. This method is known as 'induction', the establishing of a theory by reference to a large number of observed cases.

'Inductivism' has been under considerable attack in this century, and a revised version of scientific method put forward by Karl Popper has tended to replace it as an account of what scientists actually do. (24, Ch. 2) Popper's version is that, for one of any number of reasons, usually preoccupation with a problem, and generally in advance of any systematic collection of evidence, the scientist frames a hypothesis, H. He then makes a deductive inference, D, from the hypothesis: if H is the case then under certain specified conditions there will be certain discernible consequences. The next move is not, as might be expected, to look for these consequences but rather to look for a situation where, given the specified conditions, these consequences do *not* occur. The inductivist case was that the hypothesis is gradually established by an accumulation of positive evidence, all pointing to the generalisation. Popper points out that no amount of positive evidence can establish a hypothesis as true. All that positive evidence can do is give support to the hypothesis, to show, for example, that all the gases examined so far have expanded when heated, that all rooks so far observed have been black. But this does not tell us about 'all gases' or 'all rooks', and it is always possible that future evidence may upset the generalisation. What is more significant, from a methodological point of view, is a failure to discover a negative instance. The observation of ten million black rooks would not verify the hypothesis that all rooks are black, whereas one non-black rook would conclusively falsify it, and one instance of a gas which did not expand when heated would falsify the hypothesis that all gases do. So, Popper claims, the purpose of experiment and observation is not the piling up of positive evidence so much as the discovery of counter evidence, if there is any. Popper's point is that the strength of a scientific hypothesis lies in its *not* being refuted when every opportunity of refutation has been allowed.

From this highly simplified account we may extract the structure of a descriptive, explanatory theory and indicate the procedure leading to its validation. It may be put this way:

(1) Initial hypothesis H.   'all Ps are Qs.'

(2) Deduction from H: 'if all Ps are Qs then, in certain
      If H then D.   conditions, R will be the case.'

(3) Testing D.   'under the specified conditions, R has never been found *not* to be the case.'

(4) Conclusion: H is   'all Ps *are* Qs.'
      provisionally established.

This formulation shows the difference between the two approaches. The inductivist does not begin with a hypothesis, but arrives at one as the result of a large number of observations of Ps which are Qs. But, as was noted above, a hypothesis cannot be established as true in this way, the observations cannot guarantee the conclusion. The account set out above throws the emphasis on the fact of non-falsification. Scientific theories are not *proved* to be true. They may be shown to be false, by the production of counter evidence; they may be *assumed* to be true only in the absence of evidence which refutes them, where this evidence has been genuinely and systematically sought for.

One other important point about scientific method may be noted. A scientific theory rests upon certain assumptions that the scientist must take for granted. Certain initial conditions must be held to exist. In setting up experiments and making observations the scientist has to assume that the world is uniform in its operation. If P has the characteristic Q today then it has to be assumed that, in like circumstances, it will have this characteristic tomorrow. Unless he assumes this the scientist can't operate at all, since observation and experiment would be useless, either to support or to refute a hypothesis. Granted this initial assumption of uniformity in nature and the further assumption that everything that occurs has a cause, the scientist can go on to make other assumptions about the behaviour of phenomena, hypotheses that is, and subject them to scrutiny and experimental testing.

iii *Structure of practical theory*

We may now examine, by comparison, the structure of a practical theory. This will differ from a descriptive, explanatory theory in that its conclusion will normally be a prescription, or, more likely, a number of prescriptions, whereas a scientific theory will usually involve a generalised conclusion of fact. It should be clear that anyone who wanted to frame and establish a practical theory would have to go about it in a way rather different from that of the scientist. One would have to begin, not with the supposition that some possible state of affairs is so, but that there is some possible state of affairs which *ought* to be so, some desirable end to be brought about. A practical theory must begin with aims or objectives. Then one would have to ascertain what, in the given circumstances, were the best means of bringing about this desirable end, and the theory would consist in the presentation of the end to be achieved and in recommending these various means as the way to realise it. A practical theory would consist mainly of a set of recommendations supported by reasons. Its structure, then, in simplified form would be:

(1) P is desirable as an end.
(2) In the circumstances, Q is the most effective way of achieving P.
(3) Therefore, do whatever Q involves.

In practice, doing Q would involve doing all sorts of things, depending on the nature of the theory. For an educational theory, Q would break down into an indefinite number of pedagogical activities, teaching, managing children, motivating them, encouraging them and so on.

It is one thing, however, to formulate a practical theory: it is another thing to establish it as valid, or reject it as inadequate. Again, it is clear that if one wanted to validate a practical theory one could not set about it simply in the way in which a scientist validates a scientific theory. If, for example, the conclusion of the theory is 'Do xyz', there would be little point in looking at the world to see if in fact anyone *does* do xyz, or whether most people do, or if no-one does. There would be no point in trying to pile up positive instances of practice, nor in looking for negative instances either. What people actually do, or do not do, has often very little connection with what they ought to do, and no evidence about what they do in fact do will help to establish the validity of the prescription. The two sorts of theory are quite different in this respect. Whereas a descriptive theory stands or falls by the way the empirical world is, a practical theory is neither established nor refuted simply by reference to the empirical world. To validate it we should have to show that its conclusions are worthy of putting into practice. Just how this is to be done is a complex matter and we shall deal with it later in this chapter, in connection with the justification of a particular type of practical theory—theory of education.

What emerges from this account of a practical theory amounts to this: As the scientist must begin with certain assumptions as the basis of his theory, so anyone who frames a practical theory must also work with certain assumptions. The scientist's assumptions take the form of hypotheses about the empirical world. The practical theorist's assumptions involve a prescriptive hypothesis— that some end should be achieved, and assumptions about the means to achieve that end. And as the scientist must make some assumptions about initial conditions, about the raw materials he deals with —that the world is uniform in its operation and causally determined —so too the practical theorist has to make assumptions about his initial conditions, or raw materials. Of course, he too has to make assumptions about the uniformity of nature and universal causation, but he has to make other initial assumptions as well. One such assumption is that people are *able* to do whatever is necessary to achieve the end in view. There would be no point in prescribing a course of action unless it is the kind of thing that people are able to do.

iv *Assumptions in educational theory*

We can now examine more closely the particular kind of practical theory that interests us, namely, educational theory. A general theory of education will have the structure of a practical theory as set out above; that is, granted that some educational end is desirable, then certain procedures are recommended to bring that end about. This will involve certain assumptions about the end to be achieved, about those who are to be educated, and about the methods to be used in educating them. The general assumption about those to whom the prescription is addressed, that they are able to do what is prescribed, has already been mentioned.

First there will be an assumption about the end or ends. Education is a social device to realise certain ends considered desirable, and to formulate those ends is to set out what are usually called 'aims' of education. So, any general theory of education will involve such assumptions of value. Historically, educational theorists have begun from different assumptions under this heading, and this has to a large extent determined the differences between one theory and another. Some of these differences will be looked at in the next chapter. In general, however, past educational theorists have formulated aims both in terms of certain types of individuals to be produced by education and of certain types of society to be realised. The connection between these two notions, of ideal individual and ideal society, is complicated and will not be explored here. All that needs to be said here is that some theorists have seen education as producing individuals who will live in society as it is, whilst not ruling out the possibility that they will influence it for good, whereas others have seen education as aiming at an ideal society in which educated men may take their proper places. John Locke, for example, a seventeenth-century philosopher, assumed that the aim of education was to produce a responsible, civilised, Christian gentleman, who would be able to live well in the society of his day. In Locke's case the emphasis was mainly on the making of an individual. On the other hand, Plato, writing in the fifth century BC, may be said to begin with the notion of an ideal society, with education as a means of bringing this ideal society about. This too would involve making a distinct type of individual, a 'just' man, but here the emphasis tends to be on the civic or social rather than on the individualistic aspects of education. Within these limits, however, all general theories of education will start from assumptions in respect of aims to be achieved, which imply the making of a certain type of man. An associated assumption in each case is that the end proposed is one possible of realisation.

A second assumption, or set of assumptions, will concern the nature of those who are to be educated, children or pupils in general. One fundamental assumption here is that human behaviour is to some extent plastic, that what is done to children in teaching them will have some lasting effect on them. If children were born with fixed behaviour patterns and nothing that happened to them subsequently made any difference to their responses, education would have no point or meaning. Given this basic assumption of plasticity it is possible to make other, widely different assumptions about children. One can assume that they are chronically wayward creatures who, left to themselves, will be up to mischief, so that there is constant need of adult direction and control. One can go further and assume that this waywardness is not merely accidental but is built in to the child's nature, that they are born with a streak of original sin. Alternatively, one can assume, as did Rousseau, and some of his followers that children are naturally good. 'Everything', says Rousseau, 'is good as it leaves the hand of its Maker,' (38) the implication being that if children turn out badly it is because they have been spoiled. A similar view was held by Froebel, who saw the child as a living manifestation of a divine pattern, a being whose purpose it is to develop towards a pre-ordained perfection. Assumptions like these are, of course, not the only ones which could be made. Indeed it will be argued that they are not particularly helpful assumptions to make; but they are assumptions which have been made and which have had an influence on educational thinking in the past. The important point, however, is that a general theory of education will need to make *some* assumptions about children if it is to make any serious recommendations about how they should be taught and to what end.

Lastly, the realising of an educational aim will involve producing a person equipped to live in a certain style, to respond in a distinctive way to the world about him, and this has generally been understood as requiring the initiation of the pupil into certain kinds of knowledge and skill. So a third set of assumptions built in to any general theory of education will be those about the nature of knowledge and the methods considered appropriate to teach it. One assumption here is that knowledge is possible. This may seem obviously true but it is an assumption none the less, and there have been philosophers who have been concerned on this score. Few teachers perhaps would have serious doubts about the possibility of knowledge, but there can be, and have been, differing opinions about the value and reliability of what is claimed as knowledge. Plato, for example, thought that the only knowledge worthy of the name was akin to mathematical knowledge, since only here could one have certainty. All else, he thought, was mere opinion, more or less unreliable. Others, like John Dewey, tended to regard scientific knowledge as most worthwhile, since this alone gives men control over their environments and the quality of their lives. It is plain that assumptions about the nature of knowledge are likely to influence any practical recommendations made. It will, for instance, make a considerable difference to one's views of pedagogy whether one holds that knowledge is a matter of several distinct disciplines, each with its own conceptual apparatus and procedures, or whether, on the contrary, one holds that any attempt to divide knowledge into distinct compartments is unrealistic and that knowledge, like experience, is more or less undifferentiated. Then again, the *kind* of knowledge which is regarded as fundamentally important will have a bearing on the kind of methods recommended. If mathematical knowledge is held to be the basic type of knowledge there will be a tendency to recommend methods which require this characteristic type of thinking, emphasising the importance of working by deductive inference from first principles and so trying to assimilate all subjects to mathematics so far as methodology is concerned. Where physical science is regarded as the fundamental type of knowledge, there will tend to be an emphasis on methods involving observation, experiment and discovery. No-one, of course, is likely to recommend that *all* pedagogy should follow mathematical lines or scientific lines, to the exclusion of other modes of thinking, but an emphasis on one approach rather than another may be the result of different assumptions about the nature of knowledge. Another complication is that knowledge and skill may be assumed to be valuable both as a means to some external end and for their own sake. Mathematics, for example, is useful for making complicated calculations in engineering practice, but it is also a body of knowledge which may be studied simply as an intellectual discipline. Differing emphases on this point will produce different theoretical outlooks in education. What is important here, however, is that any general educational theory will inevitably involve assumptions about what is to be learned and the most effective ways of learning and teaching it.

v   *Two models of education*

Different assumptions about children and the nature of knowledge have contributed to polarisation of attitudes about education which has given rise to what are usually called the 'traditional' and the child-centred or 'progressive' approaches. (30) The traditional approach rests upon the assumption that children are more or less disinclined towards education, so that teaching them is largely a matter of direction, compulsion and restraint. The pupil, it is thought, has to be brought to terms with his education, and it is the task of the schoolmaster to bring this about. Those who favour this model usually emphasise *what* is to be learned, holding that education involves the pupil in acquiring important knowledge and skills. Moreover this knowledge is usually seen as consisting of a number of distinct areas of understanding—mathematics, science, history and so on—all of which need to be taught and learned as distinct disciplines. Education is thus represented as a sort of transaction between a full and an empty vessel. The teacher is a full man, a repository of socially important knowledge and skills and attitudes, whereas the pupil is empty and needs to be filled up. Since the pupil is usually naughty as well as empty the transaction often needs to be accompanied by the exercise of authority and force. The typical methods will be those of instruction and demonstration by the teacher, with passive reception and imitation by the pupil. As the only source of educational advantage to the pupil will be the teacher, attention to him is required at all times, co-operation between one pupil and another being on the whole discouraged. This account is a caricature, perhaps, but it is recognisable as depicting the kind of situation which might have been found in an elementary school at the end of the nineteenth century and may still be found, occasionally, in schools today.

What is called the 'progressive' or 'child-centred' approach, characteristic of most infant and junior schools today, rests on a different set of assumptions. Here the child is usually assumed to be fundamentally well-disposed towards education, with spontaneous impulses of curiosity and interest. It is assumed, too, that knowledge and skill are important because they provide a means by which the child may develop his potentialities and 'grow' from within. Education is regarded not merely as a one-way transaction between a teacher and a pupil, a handing-over of knowledge, but rather as a co-operative enterprise in which the pupil is encouraged to take the initiative, to explore his environment, to find things out for himself, the teacher providing the help needed to ensure that the child gets the necessary intellectual stimulation and opportunities for development. Traditional teaching and instruction, the formal classroom situation, give way to free-ranging enquiry; discovery methods and exploratory activity by the pupil are encouraged, as is co-operation in learning between one pupil and another. Underlying this view is the notion that, as the child's experience is not differentiated into rigid compartments called 'mathematics', 'science' and the like, so too 'knowledge' is not a matter of rigidly separated disciplines and should not be treated as though it were. Progressive educationalists tend to avoid traditional subject divisions and a compartmentalised curriculum, and think rather in terms of 'integrated' activities. Here we have, then, two prototypes of an educational theory, each involving different assumptions about children and about knowledge and methods as a basis for what is recommended for practice. Taken in conjunction with some declared aim, some notion as to what is to count as an educated man, each would qualify, in a broad sense, as a general theory of education. We shall find that the historically important theories we shall deal with tend to approximate to one or other of these two models.

vi Justifying an educational theory

We come now to the crucial question of justification. How are we to put an educational theory as such to the test, to discover whether it is valid or invalid, whether its recommendations should be adopted or not? The testing of a scientific theory presents little difficulty in principle. A scientific theory purports to give information about the empirical world, and it will be accepted or rejected simply according to whether what it says fits in with the facts of the empirical world. Educational theories, as practical theories, do not set out to give information of this kind but to say what should be done. So, to criticise or reject an educational theory we should have to show not simply that its prescriptive conclusions were unacceptable, although if they *were* unacceptable for any reason this would count decisively against the theory, but that these conclusions were not justifiable in terms of the assumptions made, or that the assumptions themselves were open to question. The doubts which have been cast on the claim of educational theory to be theory at all came because it was thought that educational theories were not really open to criticisms of this kind, or not very clearly so. Our analysis of the structure of a practical theory in general and of educational theory as a species of practical theory indicates how such criticism might be forthcoming. Of course, it also indicates the way in which such a theory might be supported, but it is important to stress the role of criticism here. As the strength of an established scientific theory lies in the fact that it is open to criticism but has survived all attempts to refute it, so it is essential to the standing of an educational theory as such that it should be possible to criticise it, and that it should be able to stand up to such criticism. A theory which is not open to criticism is not open to confirmation either, so it is important that we should be able to set out ways in which a general theory of education might be open to attack.

One way would be to show that, granted the truth of the various assumptions involved in it, there was some inconsistency in the argument based on them. A theory which accepted the assumptions of the traditional model regarding children and methods could hardly prescribe a policy of 'soft' pedagogy, with relaxed discipline and free-and-easy methods, without leaving itself open to the charge of inconsistency. Similarly it would be inconsistent to claim that the pupils' immediate interests and impulses are of paramount importance in education and go on to recommend practices which would ensure that children would learn despite their actual and immediate lack of interest in what was being taught. A theory, that is, could be faulted for lack of internal coherence. Or it might be shown that the assumptions themselves were faulty in some way. Assumptions about the nature of children and about the effectiveness of methods would involve some reference to empirical fact, and it might be possible to show that these supposedly factual assumptions were false, or were untestable. Assumptions about children might be contradicted by the experimentally established conclusions of those who, like Piaget, have studied children and their development; or it might be shown that it is impossible to decide rationally whether they are true or false. Froebel's assumption that children develop according to some divine pattern is an example of this last point. Froebel seems to be making a factual assumption here, but it is difficult to see how it could ever be shown to be either true or false. No observation of actual children would settle the matter one way or another. A theory which rested on untestable assumptions like this would be hardly more acceptable than one based on assumptions which could be shown to be false. The reason why incorrect or untestable assumptions about children are objectionable here is that they may lead to the holding of unrealistic aims, or the recommending of inappropriate methods. It is only fair to say that as far as methods go this need not necessarily be the case. The connections between the various assumptions and the practical conclusions are not, logically, very tight, and dubious assumptions about children could go along with pedagogical recommendations which were quite valuable in practice. This discrepancy would however vitiate the theory as a theory because of its lack of internal coherence.

Again it might be possible to show that the assumptions about the effectiveness of methods were, in fact, ill-founded. The effectiveness of methods like 'Look and Say' or 'Projects' or 'Discovery' can be tested and any educational theory which recommended methods which could be shown to be ineffective could be criticised and rejected on these grounds. So too could a theory which recommended methods about which it was impossible to discover whether they were effective or not. If there is no rational way of deciding whether or not a child develops according to a divine pattern, there will be no way of deciding whether methods purportedly designed to bring about this development are effective either. Yet another possible ground of criticism would be that the methods recommended, whether effective or not, were in some way harmful to the child, or immoral.

A theory might also be criticised because its assumptions about the nature of knowledge were faulty—if, for example, it was based on the belief that all knowledge is basically mathematical, or that the only kind of knowledge possible is scientific knowledge, or the knowledge of God. Criticism here would be based on what a philosopher would call an epistemological point, that there is no good reason to suppose that there are not other forms of knowledge besides mathematics or science, and to assert that all knowledge is of God is to maintain what cannot be shown to be true or false. It might also be argued that what was assumed to be knowledge was not really knowledge at all, or that, as knowledge, it was of little value, intrinsically or instrumentally. A theory which prescribed studies in astrology would be open to criticism on the first count, and one which laid stress on the intricacies of, say, heraldry would be vulnerable on the second.

Lastly, an educational theory could be criticised in respect of its assumptions about aims. The possibilities of argument here are considerable and we shall deal with this topic again in Chapter 4. We can, however, indicate here some ways in which criticism could be made at this level. A theory might be rejected because its aims rested on assumptions about the nature of man which were false, or untestable. This point has already been made concerning assumptions about children as the raw material of education, but a wider issue is involved here. Aims in education invariably rest on some notion of what man, as such, is like, or could be like, and an educational aim may simply be the realisation of this 'true nature' of man. A theory, therefore, which based its aim on some questionable assumption about men, that they are perfectible, for example, might be open to the charge that this assumption was false, or untestable. A theory might also be objected to on the grounds that its aim could not possibly be realised, if it aimed at making men immortal, for example. It would also be possible to object to a theory by arguing that the type of individual aimed at was morally unacceptable. The making of a Nietzschean superman with unsympathetic views about the rights and feelings of inferiors could be attacked on moral grounds.

This last example raises some difficulty, as would a similar point about methods. Where assumptions of fact are at issue we may fault them by showing the facts to be otherwise. Where assumptions are untestable, this may be pointed out. It is much more difficult to contest assumptions concerning values, either in respect of ends or methods. To do this would involve showing that the assumptions complained of are incompatible with other assumptions which may be made and ought to be made—that we ought to prefer equality, or kindness, or respect for individuals, to self-interest or power or political success, or efficiency even. Criticisms of this kind are far more difficult to establish than those which can appeal to the empirical facts of the world. None the less an educational theory might be criticised and rejected simply on the grounds that its aims were morally objectionable.

vii *Summary*

Educational theory, it has been maintained, is a species of practical theory, an argument whose conclusion consists of recommendations for practice. Its structure contains certain assumptions, about the desirability of ends, about the nature of men and of children, and about knowledge and pedagogical methods, and it is on the basis of

24

these assumptions that its practical recommendations are made. Understanding this structure enables us to see how such a theory might be put to the test. A scientific theory can be shown to be inadequate if it contains false assumptions about the way the world is. An educational theory could be shown to be inadequate if its assumptions are faulty, either false as a matter of fact, or untestable, or incompatible with accepted moral principles, or if its recommendations are inconsistent with its assumptions. In other words, an educational theory is a logically complex structure and can be assessed in a number of different ways. In so far as it contains empirical assertions it can be checked by reference to empirical facts; in so far as it involves value judgments it may be vulnerable to philosophical arguments; in so far as it is an argument it can be tested for internal coherence. If it fails in any of these respects it may be rejected as a guide to practice.

On the other hand, if an educational theory can be criticised it is possible that it may be defended and its conclusions established as worthy of acceptance in practice. This could be done by showing that its aims were capable of being realised and morally acceptable, that its assumptions about pupils were supported by appropriate evidence, and that no exception could be taken to its assumptions about the nature of knowledge and the appropriateness of methods. In other words the theory could be validated by showing it to be rationally defensible. This accords with the Popperian methodology mentioned earlier. A valid educational theory is one which can withstand attempts to reject it on the grounds that its assumptions, arguments or conclusions are in some way unacceptable. If it does withstand such criticism then, in so far as anyone accepts the aims written into it, the practical conclusions set out what ought to be done. Thus the question of academic integrity raised in Chapter 1 would seem to be answered. It is not true that educational theory, in the sense of general theory, is theory only by courtesy, a kind of pseudo-theory. It is theory in its own right and by exposing itself to the possibility of criticism and rejection it qualifies as theory no less than theories of other kinds. There may be, of course, indefensible theories of education, as there are indefensible theories in science. Not all educational theories may be able to stand up to the kinds of criticism outlined above. But there is nothing in principle about a general theory of education which justifies the withdrawal of title from it. There are rational procedures for rejecting or confirming an educational theory, and this establishes for it a good claim to our attention. This point will be important when, in Chapter 6, we discuss the possibility of an on-going, contemporary, general theory of education.

3

Historical theories of education

i *Introduction*

In Chapter 2 we looked at the structure of an educational theory and said that it involved a number of assumptions, about aims, pupils, knowledge and methods. The point was made that, whilst the structure of an educational theory is fixed, different assumptions will result in different theories with different recommendations for practice. We shall now try to exemplify this by outlining some historically important theories of education and bringing out the various assumptions made in each of them. This will enable us to see how far these historical theories are open to criticism and to indicate how a study of them might be useful to teachers and others. This chapter will be concerned with presenting these theories; criticism of them, and some suggestions about the way in which they could contribute to an understanding of contemporary educational issues will be given in the next chapter.

A preliminary matter might be dealt with here. Some theories of education explicitly aim at producing an individual to fit into an existing social context, an educated man for the society of the day. In others the situation is more complicated. A theory of the overarching kind may offer two related positions; first, that, ideally, society ought to be ordered in a certain way; and, secondly, that the individual to be aimed *at*, the educated man, is one able to take his place in the ideal society prescribed. The position may be further complicated in that the writer may not explicitly postulate the nature of his ideal society, but rather assume it in his recommendations. An educational theory, then, may often be best understood in terms of a social or political theory, directly or indirectly connected with it. Plato's educational ideas are closely connected with his views about an ideal society. Rousseau moves somewhat ambiguously between a concern for producing an individual for an existing, imperfect society and producing one for an ideal society yet to come. Dewey's educational theory undoubtedly points to a certain kind of society, a modern democracy. It is, therefore, sometimes necessary to distinguish between the explicit, declared aims of a theory and what might be called its implicit or undeclared aims, those which may lie beneath the positive recommendations made. Educational theories, like political theories, are sometimes close to being propaganda, and we need to be aware of this.

ii *The educational theory of Plato*

The main educational doctrines of Plato are to be found in two of his longer dialogues, *The Republic* and *The Laws*. Only the educational theory of *The Republic* will be dealt with here. This does not mean that what Plato says about education in *The Laws* and elsewhere is unimportant. In *The Laws*, for example, Plato sets out in some detail recommendations for the education of young children, an important topic not discussed at length in *The Republic*. Since, however, the purpose of this chapter is to illustrate as economically as possible various large-scale theories, *The Republic* is the most convenient work of Plato's to deal with, since in this dialogue the various key assumptions made are most easily identified. In *The Republic* Plato is, amongst other things, concerned with an analysis of the nature of 'justice' and with what is involved in the notion of a just man. The word 'just' is not an altogether adequate translation of the word Plato uses. The sense of the term would be better expressed as 'moral' or 'right-living', and Plato's main question as: 'What constitutes "right-living" in men?' To answer this Plato sketches the institution of an ideal city-state, on the grounds that justice in the individual is analogous to justice in the state, and that we shall better grasp what justice is if we see it writ large, in social terms. Plato's conclusion, put briefly, is that the just state is one in which the various social orders which compose it, the farmers and craftsmen, the soldiers, the rulers, are organised in a hierarchical way, the rulers ruling the city, the soldiers guarding it, and the remainder providing it with economic services, each social class and each individual performing the social role appropriate to it and to him. A state ordered in this way, Plato maintains, would be balanced and healthy, 'right-living' and so just. A just state is a socially harmonious whole. (34)

A similar hierarchical model is involved in the notion of a just man. The individual man, like the state, is held to be composed of different aspects or orders. Man is a creature with appetites, with spirited passions and a capacity for reflection. These aspects of the human personality correspond to the social orders in the state:

27

the appetites correspond to the producers, the spirited part to the soldiers, and the rational, reflective part to the rulers. And, according to Plato, as the state is just when each part of the social order keeps its place and performs its proper duties, so the 'just' man will be one who is so ordered that his appetites and his passions are subordinated to the control of his 'higher' nature, his rational, reflective part. The just man is thus a microcosm of the just state. Whenever this hierarchical ordering is disturbed, either in the state or in man, the organism is sick or 'unjust'. If the soldiers or the workers try to usurp the functions of the rulers, the state is disordered, giving way to imperfect forms of society, to timocracy in the first case, democracy in the second. By analogy, if the individual is ruled by his bodily appetites, or by his passions, rather than by reason, the man is no longer 'right-living', but is morally disordered, or 'unjust'.

Here we have a social theory of a practical kind, giving recommendations about what is to count as justice and what steps need to be taken to secure it. Embedded in this social theory is an educational theory directed towards the production of 'just' men, but more particularly towards the making of those who are to govern the ideal state, the rulers or Guardians. Plato is not much concerned in *The Republic* with the education of the lowest social order, the craftsmen, farmers and merchants. They are to have a training in literacy, with some moral instructions to make them obedient servants of the state and to fulfil their proper roles. They will then be left to pick up their crafts and callings in the traditional way. Plato's main concern in *The Republic* is with higher education, with the training of the future rulers.

To understand Plato's educational recommendations we need to look at his general philosophical position. Plato held that 'reality' involved two distinct orders of existence. One is the everyday world of appearances, the phenomenal world of objects and qualities which we experience through the senses. Plato thought this world attractive but unreliable, a world of constant change, and held that we could have no real knowledge of what was so transient, only opinion. Behind this confusing world of appearances is another, ideal world, made up of what Plato calls the 'Forms' or 'Types'. The constitution and status of this other world are left vague, but it may be understood as consisting of an indefinite number of perfect, eternal, changeless entities, patterns, of which the ephemeral things of the phenomenal world are imperfect copies. There are many individual men in the phenomenal world, but what makes them men is that they are all copies of the Form of Man. Individual men grow old and die but the Form of Man does not change. Likewise, there are the Forms of the Beautiful, the Just, the State . . . a Form for every general term we have. Beautiful things are beautiful because they copy the Form of the Beautiful, just actions are just because they reflect the Form of Justice, and so on. The Forms themselves are supposed to be ordered in a hierarchy, with the Form of the 'Good' at the apex. Plato holds that, in so far as knowledge is possible, it must be of this world of Forms, since only here can we have the grasp of true reality, of certainty, which he supposes to be the essence of knowledge, as distinct from mere opinion. (14, Ch. 2)

We may now look at the assumptions which underlie Plato's theory of education. He makes assumptions about the end to be achieved, about the nature of those who are to be educated, and about the nature of knowledge and the efficacy of certain methods. He assumes as an over-riding aim the production of a certain type of man, the just man, and a certain type of state, the just society, in which just men will find and keep their proper places. A just man is one trained and willing to fulfil his role in society. But, although ideally every man in society would be just in this sense, within the category of just men there will be some who are marked off from the others by having superior abilities. Plato's assumption about human beings in general is that they are entities consisting of a perishable body linked with a soul, one part of which, the rational part, is immortal. Of the two aspects the soul is the more important, and different men have souls of different degrees of quality. Some souls have more of the rational, the noble, than others. Some men, as Plato puts it, have gold in their souls, others have souls of iron and bronze, inferior souls. The psychology here is crude and not altogether clear, but what is clear is that Plato is primarily concerned with the education of those who have superior qualities, souls of gold. Education, whilst not neglecting the training of the body, ultimately has to do with the correct nurturing of the soul, turning its attention away from the world of mere appearances towards the understanding of the world of Forms, and particularly the Form of the Good. To achieve this end, Plato assumes that certain procedures will be effective. The educational programme recommended for those who are to become, first the soldiers and then the rulers, involves different regimes to correspond with different stages in the individual's development. At the lowest levels of awareness, in childhood, his life is mainly appetitive and centred on the world of appearances. At this stage his senses are to be trained, to instil in him a love of beauty and order and harmony. Then the spirited part of the soul is to be fed with stories of heroes and noble lives, to fire him with moral fervour and a desire to live well. This goes along with a period of military service in which physical and intellectual training is continued under the most rigorous conditions, the young warriors living communally and having no property or family life of their own. Then, those who show themselves fitted for it begin a study which will open the way to true knowledge, knowledge of the world of Forms. This, Plato thinks, must involve acquaintance with the mathematical sciences, arithmetic and geometry, which will turn the pupils' attention away from the world of appearances, towards the underlying, orderly, structure of things which mathematics reflects. Plato's point is that when we study, say, geometry, we are not really concerned with the material lines and shapes, the triangles on paper, but with 'real' objects, mathematical objects which these visual aids presuppose. These 'mathematical objects' are entities similar to, but inferior to, the Forms themselves. Mathematics is thus a 'bridge' study, leading from the world of appearances to the world of reality. Again, this study of mathematics corresponds to a higher stage in the individual's development, a sort of half-way house between a concentration on appearances and a rational grasp of the non-phenomenal world. Plato illustrates this by the simile of 'The Line' in Book 6 of *The Republic* where there is a progression from mere illusion, through beliefs about the physical world, to mathematical reasoning as a prelude to the highest mode of intellectual awareness, an intuition of the Forms themselves. There is an interesting analogy here in the account given by Piaget, who sees the child as developing from a pre-rational stage, through a stage centred on sensory experiences and on to a stage of formal operations not tied closely to sense experience. In Plato, when this mathematical training is completed the pupil enters into the study of a kind of philosophy, akin to mathematics and logic, called 'dialectic', which operates, in a way not clearly specified, on the Forms themselves, and culminates in a grasp of the highest Form of all, the Form of the Good. The assumption here is that to know the Form of the Good is to be equipped with true knowledge, with a certain grasp of reality from which all other knowledge can be derived. Thus the possessor of this ultimate knowledge will unerringly know what is good and the reason why it is so. The philosopher, for such he will have become, will be able to apply this knowledge, especially to the ruling of the state. The Guardians will thus be philosophers, educated to the highest degree of rationality, and fitted to rule because they alone will *know* what is good and just and wise. The other orders in the state will not *know* in this sense, and will need to have their opinions guided by those who do.

Plato's educational recommendations then, are: Select the most intelligent and bravest, those who have souls of gold, and educate them according to the different stages of their development, giving them first a sense of the harmony and order which underlies the sensible world, and then by rigorous formal studies turning their souls away from the errors and confusions of the world of sense to grasp the truth, the knowledge of true reality. Only in this way, by being ruled by those who understand, will the state be made, and kept, just. Such are Plato's declared aims and recommendations. It would, however, be appropriate here to ask: 'What are the undeclared aims? What is Plato really recommending here?' To answer this we have to put *The Republic* into historical perspective. Plato lived in a time of great unrest. The defeat of Athens by Sparta was followed by an increase in the power of the Athenian people, who challenged the established order in the city. Plato, who belonged to the Athenian aristocracy, was apprehensive of such democratic power, hence his ready assumption that the best kind of society was one in which the different social orders keep their places. Plato's declared rationale for this was that such a state would reflect the Good, with harmony in the body politic. If we accept this and accept the rule of an élite as analogous to the rule of reason in the soul, then, on Plato's terms, we have the equation of a just society with an aristocratic society, a society ruled by the 'best'. Plato's educational views were thus a reflection of his social and political sympathies. *The Republic* offers an educational theory presented in the most persuasive terms: it aims at producing just men in a just society. What it does in fact is to recommend an aristocratic, elitist order based on what are held to be fundamental differences in men, and gives a recipe for achieving such an order. This is not, as such, a criticism of the theory. It may be that in Plato's day an elitist solution was the best available, as it may be argued that it is today. But such a case needs to be argued. It is not self-evidently true: the underlying assumptions need to be brought out and established and the arguments submitted to scrutiny. In Plato's theory there is an assumption about ends, about the kind of social order desirable. Acceptance of the educational theory involves acceptance of this assumption. One is not, of course, obliged to accept it.

iii   *The educational theory of Rousseau*

Rousseau's most important contribution to educational theory is to be found in his *Émile*, published in 1762. Rousseau was a controversial, sometimes confused and often confusing writer whose influence on European thinking has none the less been original and stimulating. It is impossible to do justice to his work in a short space and what follows is no more than an outline. Perhaps the best way of bringing out the significance of his educational theorising is to relate it to his social philosophy as a whole. It must be realised, however, that Rousseau's thinking and writing is complex and controversial and that more than one interpretation of his views is possible.

Rousseau belonged to the generation which preceded the French Revolution of 1789 and he is prominent amongst the writers and thinkers who prepared the intellectual climate for that great upheaval. His writings, though intensely personal and individualistic, were very much connected with the social developments of his time. These developments, put briefly and with all the disadvantages of compression and oversimplification, could be said to spring from the change from a semi-feudal nation-state to a modern industrial-type society moving towards democracy. France in the mid-eighteenth century was beginning to anticipate the social and industrial development which was to come in the nineteenth century. The autocratic regime established by Louis XIV was beginning to feel the social strains which were eventually to break it apart. But this is hardly how Rousseau would have seen the situation or his part in it. The distinction between declared and undeclared, unconscious aims is pronounced in Rousseau's work. He probably saw himself as something other than one of the spokesmen of the new order about to be born, and he put the matter in rather different terms. He was none the less a severe critic of French society of his day, holding it to be corrupt and unjust, and one of his most important books, *The Social Contract* (1762), may be regarded as an attempt to point the way towards the political regeneration of society. *The Social Contract* was a plea for a new kind of society, based upon the real interests of all its members as opposed to one based on aristocratic privilege; specifically, it tries to deal with the problem of how men can secure the real and substantial benefits of social life without losing their individual freedom as men. Exactly what relation *Émile* bears to *The Social Contract* is a matter for debate, but the position may be put, not too misleadingly, as follows: *The Social Contract* takes men as they are and tries to answer the question: 'What political arrangements are needed to bring about a better society, where freedom and order are both secured?' *Émile* takes laws and social arrangements as they are and tries to answer the question: 'What kind of man could live well even in this society, and how is he to be produced?' Taken together the two works amount to a more or less coherent attempt at providing a programme for a new society, and a new kind of man, one who could live well in the new society as well as in the old. Rousseau is thus not to be regarded simply as an educational reformer. His educational theory is to a large extent complementary to his political writings. In these Rousseau advocates what amounts to a democratic form of government based on what he calls the General Will, the rational will of all the members of the state, and a society composed of independent citizens, with a widespread ownership of property. As a corollary of this political aim he advocated freedom of thought, simplicity in social life, independence and individualism in men. Émile, the hero of Rousseau's educational programme, is to be brought up with what Marxists would call the 'bourgeois' virtues.

This, or something like this, is the undeclared aim of the educational theory—the making of the bourgeois citizen, the middle-class man of the new social order. The declared aim is put somewhat differently. In *Émile*, Rousseau does not call for the making of a bourgeois citizen as such. Instead, he appeals for a 'return to nature', and his educational theory is often represented as a 'naturalist' revolt against formalism. Rousseau advocates, not bourgeois man, but what he sometimes calls the 'natural' man, and the educational policy he offers is one 'according to nature'. Now in dealing with this slogan we are in some difficulty since the term 'nature' is one of considerable ambiguity and Rousseau uses it in more than one way. Consequently students of Rousseau have to do a good deal of interpretation to bring out at all clearly what his message is, and there is always the possibility that his meaning may be misinterpreted or misunderstood.

Rousseau's claim is that education should be 'according to nature', and Émile is to be the 'natural man'. Several things may be meant by this, but for the moment we will deal with only two of them.

By 'nature' may be meant the way things are in the world of sense experience. This is nature in the sense in which rocks and trees, sunshine and rain are a part of nature, the sense in which a child is a natural object. In this case, to follow nature would be to treat the child as a human animal, according to the laws of its growth, the development of its various faculties, its maturation. No doubt this is at least partly what Rousseau meant. He wanted to concentrate attention on the child as a child. He reacted strongly against the eighteenth century fashion of treating children as though they were little adults and childhood as an inconvenient period of imperfection to be disguised and got through as quickly as possible. Rousseau points out that children are not adults, certainly not miniature adults. They do not think as adults do, nor do they have the same needs, interests or concerns as adults; they should not be regarded as imperfect adults or treated as such. Rousseau, it has been said, 'discovered the child', emphasising that childhood was a distinct and important part of the individual's life, with its own peculiar development, its own typical ways of thinking and feeling, and its own perfection. Child-rearing, he thought, should be a matter of respecting the child's nature as a growing, developing being, to enable it to reach the perfection of childhood. Childhood should be a time when the child lived a life of sensations rather than of knowledge, a life of experience through the senses, a period of coming to terms with the natural world about him. It was not a time for adult concerns, or even preparation for adult concerns— this would come later. Childhood was to be the 'sleep of reason', and an education according to nature would be one which recognised this and took due account of the child's life in the 'country of sensations'.

There is also, however, in Rousseau another notion which bears on this point, in which 'nature' is contrasted favourably with 'social'. Rousseau had argued in two earlier works, the *Discourse on the Sciences and the Arts* and the *Discourse on the Origin of Inequality*, that man is not improved by civilisation, and that in some pre-social 'state of nature' he was superior in goodness to the artificial, civilised man of modern society. This claim would hardly stand up to anthropological enquiry but Rousseau uses it as a hypothesis to account for the presence of evil in the world. This, he alleged, comes, not from man's original nature, which is good, but from the corruption brought about by society. This doctrine may support a belief that what is required for the regeneration of man is the removal of arbitrary social restraints, the corrupting influences of social life, so that the natural goodness of the individual may be revealed. This same doctrine may be used to underwrite an influential interpretation of Rousseau's views on child-rearing. The child is assumed to be naturally good, so that all that is needed for his upbringing is a watchful passivity by his teacher, who is not to impose adult social restraints on him but rather is there to provide opportunities for him to develop his innate goodness. There is much in Rousseau to support such a view, at least as regards the nurture of the young child. Émile is to be brought up in the country, away from the town. He is not to be taught adult moral standards, these will mean nothing to him. He is to be as free as his situation permits. He is to be controlled by his own limitations in the face of natural obstacles to his will and, so far as his real needs as a child are concerned, by the dictates of his Tutor, whose will is to seem to Émile an impersonal force like that shown by the intractable 'things' of nature. Émile is not to be restrained at this time by merely social conventions. These will have their force when he is a man, but by then his 'natural' goodness will have been developed, and even if he has to live in a corrupt society he will not be corrupted by it. He will be the 'savage who can live in the town', the natural man at home in society. (38, Bk 3) This strain in Rousseau has prompted more than one experiment in the permissive upbringing of children, with an emphasis on their innate goodness and on the perils of adult restraints on childish ways.

These views allow us to give one interpretation to Rousseau's thesis that education should be according to nature. Education, it may be said, should be natural in that it follows the child-like nature of the pupil, accommodating his nurture to his age and his real needs as a child and not to the requirements of the adult he may become. The emphasis is to be on activity by the child, on a widening of his experience, on his exploration of his environment, on the satisfaction of his present needs and interests. In Book 2 of *Émile*, Rousseau develops this idea of a practical, experiential, first-hand education. The child is to be concerned with things rather than with words, with the concrete world about him rather than with books and formalised knowledge. Everything he is required to learn is to be immediately relevant to him as a child. Education should be natural, too, in the sense that it should aim at releasing the natural man, here understood as the free, unspoiled being who is usually confined beneath the social veneer. This may well be taken as a gospel of freedom for the children, a cry for a 'negative' education, a policy of minimal restraint on the child's innate spontaneity of impulse. Interpreted in this way Rousseau's theory is 'progressive' rather than traditional, child-centred rather than teacher-centred or subject-centred. Those who have subsequently offered progressive theories of education, Pestalozzi and Froebel for example, have all been influenced by such an interpretation. Those who do not see education in 'progressive' terms have been inclined to blame Rousseau for an approach they regard as anti-intellectual, anti-social and, in so far as it is thought to play down the idea of initiating the child into traditional areas of formal knowledge, anti-educational.

A reading of Rousseau may lead to such an interpretation. But, as suggested earlier, another interpretation is possible. It may be said that it is wrong to suppose that Rousseau sees the 'natural man' simply in terms of a pre-social innocence, as a 'noble savage'. There was a view, not uncommon in the eighteenth century, that man is a perfectible being, that there is no assignable limit to his possible improvement. Man, the optimistic humanist *philosophes* of eighteenth-century France thought, is held back from perfection by his imperfect social arrangements. His condition depends entirely on his environment and its influence. This environment is alterable and, given adequate social and educational arrangements, man's future is one of continuous amelioration of his circumstances and improvement of his faculties. Education, in a broad sense, was the key to perfectibility. 'Education peut tout', declared Helvetius, one of Rousseau's contemporaries. Rousseau may be thought to subscribe to this perfectibilist view when, in the *Discourse on the Origin of Inequality* he maintains that man differs from the animals in being able to perfect himself through the development of his reason. (17, Ch. 3) So it is possible to see Rousseau's natural man as idealised man, not the uncorrupted savage of a pre-social past, but the perfected man of the future. In this case, making the natural man would not be a matter of throwing off social restraints and certainly not a matter of playing down man's intellectual heritage in the interests of a childish integrity. It would, instead, involve reconstructing, positively, on a rational basis, those social conditions necessary for a free man in an improving society, and of using the whole of man's intellectual capital to further his development. *The Social Contract, Émile,* and an 'education according to nature' make good sense on this assumption. Rousseau's theory thus interpreted would amount to the recommendation that the child should be so taught that his nature would be realised to the full, that he should become the free, morally-mature citizen, ideal man. (45, Ch. 2)

It is likely that such an interpretation is closer to what Rousseau really meant. It is certainly more consistent with the view expressed in *Émile* taken as a whole. The former interpretation with its stress on the negative approach to education gains most support from the earlier parts of the book, which deal with the education of young children. The later interpretation, which takes into account Rousseau's insistence on a change to a positive education as Émile grows older, makes sense of much that otherwise seems puzzling in Rousseau. It would absolve him from charges of inconsistency, of maintaining that men should be both 'natural men' and 'citizens', and that, whilst social influences corrupt, the adolescent Émile should none the less be schooled in that social heritage. Rousseau's message could then be given fairly simply and intelligibly. Education is the means to producing the natural man; the 'nature' referred to here is man's ideal self, the 'perfected'/man. The society which corrupts is the imperfect society of the day, which needs to be refashioned to give effect to the general will of its citizens. In the making of the natural man all the intellectual heritage of humankind is to be deployed, although, of course, it is to be made available to the pupil only in so far as it is relevant to his present needs and experience. In realising his nature as a man, his 'nature' as a child, a growing, developing being, must not be ignored.

After this somewhat compressed account of Rousseau's educational thinking we may look again at his theory in the light of the assumptions made in it. Rousseau makes an initial assumption of value, that the end of the educational process should be the 'natural man'. He makes, too, an assumption about the raw material of education, human nature, to the effect that men, or children, are born good, naturally good. He also makes the assumption that men are, in some sense, perfectible. Lastly, he makes certain assumptions about what knowledge is appropriate and what methods are best calculated to realise the end. That knowledge is appropriate which fits in with Émile's nature as a child and as a man, his nature as a growing being and as a candidate for perfectibility. Beginning with simple sensory awareness it goes on to include the traditional formalised culture of humankind, 'mathematics and science, history and philosophy, literature and religion. The methods to be recommended are those which, to begin with, encourage Émile to explore his world and to learn at first hand what he needs to know. As he gets older first hand knowledge gives way to learning from books, active exploration of the environment is supplemented by teaching about the ways of men and institutions; the simple development of the senses is followed by activities designed to develop social and moral attitudes which become a man, a husband and a citizen. On the basis of these assumptions Rousseau advocates the pedagogy of Émile, which, so far as its emphasis on child activity and respect for children goes, has brought about a revolution in educational methods since his day.

iv *The educational theory of James Mill*

The educational theory to be examined next is that of the group of early nineteenth century thinkers known as the English Utilitarians. The Utilitarians, the more important of whom were Bentham, James Mill and John Stuart Mill, were social critics and reformers of great influence. They lived when England was changing from a predominantly agricultural country to the foremost industrial country in the world, and they became deeply involved in the social and political movements which accompanied this change. With them, as with Plato and Rousseau, we can distinguish between the declared and undeclared elements in their political and social theories. England at this time was undergoing a shift from a semi-feudal kind of society in which men had traditional places and roles, to a society of 'free' and 'independent' individuals, 'free', that is, of traditional roles. A 'market economy', a competitive arena for individual energies and talents, was replacing the paternalistic regime which had lasted more or less since medieval times. In this new economic climate, an energetic and individualistic 'middle class', thrifty, prudent and industrious, was making its way, coming in time to own the coal mines and cotton mills and to sit in the reformed parliaments from 1832 onwards. It would not be greatly overstating the truth to say that the Utilitarians were the voice of this new middle class and that their social theories supported the new order. This was not always explicitly declared in their recommendations. When they advocated parliamentary, legal, economic or educational reform they did not usually refer to the desirability of establishing a middle-class society. Instead, they spoke of the need to promote the 'greatest happiness of the greatest number'. This was the celebrated 'principle of utility' which they used to measure the adequacy of any institution, law or social practice that came to their attention. If it could be shown that these things did not or were not likely to maximise the general happiness, this, the Utilitarians held, was a good reason for altering them, for repealing the law or amending the practice. They conceived of the public happiness in middle-class terms and were tireless in showing that much of the social fabric of the time was not calculated to promote such happiness. Their historical task was to bring social institutions into conformity with the changing economic conditions of their day.

The Utilitarians saw in education a powerful reforming device. Education, they realised, was a means of bringing up future generations to behave in ways likely to realise the Utilitarian ideal. Their theory of education was simple and it was set out with a brief clarity by James Mill, in the essay on 'Education' published in a supplement to the *Encyclopaedia Britannica* in 1821. (25) The theory is admirable for our present purpose since, resting on a few simple assumptions and pointing to, though not specifying in detail, pedagogical recommendations of a somewhat uncompromising kind, it reveals its basic structure in a transparent way.

Mill begins with an assumption about the aim of education. This follows from his general position, that the purpose of all rational activity ought to be to increase the amount of happiness in the world and to diminish the amount of pain. This is, for him, what politics, economics, law, morals and education are all about. The over-riding aim in education is to produce the kind of man whose actions are likely to increase, not only his own happiness, but also that of everyone who has dealings with him. The end of education, he says, is to render the human mind, as far as possible, the cause of human happiness. An educated man would be Utilitarian Man. Mill thought that such a man would have the virtues of temperance, generosity and justice, allied with what he calls 'intelligence', which includes both knowledge and sagacity, knowing about the world and being able to use that knowledge. Such virtues and accomplishments were, in fact, just those which would enable him to live well in the individualistic kind of society the Utilitarians were helping to bring about.

Mill's theory involves two important assumptions about those who are to be educated. First, that they are essentially selfish. Men can only act in such ways as they think will increase their own pleasure or avoid pain for themselves. This is the doctrine of psychological hedonism, accepted generally by the Utilitarians. Mill does not admit this doctrine explicitly in the essay, but it is to be found in other writings of his and it is implied in what he does say in the essay about human motives. The second assumption, once again implicit rather than spelt out in the essay, is that men are born intellectually empty. Their minds at birth are, metaphorically, like clean slates, or perhaps empty rooms, and need to be written on by experience, or filled up with mental furniture. This assumption comes from Locke, the seventeenth-century philosopher, and was commonly held by the empiricist philosophers of the eighteenth and nineteenth centuries. It was thought that we received 'sensations' or 'impressions' from the world outside us and that these sensations or impressions were taken into the mind, which was represented as a kind of non-spatial warehouse in which experiences could be stored, sorted and compared. Sensations or impressions could be reproduced as 'ideas', by means of the memory and the imagination. To remember was to bring out an idea from its storage place; to forget was to be unable to find some mental acquisition; to use the imagination was to join up ideas in a free and fanciful way with no necessary correspondence to the real world. We still talk in this way when we speak of a man having a 'well-stored mind', or of someone being 'empty headed', and Mr Gradgrind in Dickens's *Hard Times* echoed this assumption when he regarded the children in school as there simply to be 'filled up with facts'. The traditional model of education owes much to this view. The important point, however, is that all our ideas are thought to come to us from experience, and so the kind of ideas a man has will depend on the experiences he has.

For Mill, then, the raw material of education was an individual, essentially egoistic, who could be put in the way of sensations and ideas by a suitable manipulation of his environment and experiences.

Mill's theory also involved assumptions about the nature of knowledge and the effectiveness of pedagogical methods. With the 'clean slate' view of the mind went the doctrine that ideas tend to associate together according to the frequency with which the corresponding elements in the external world are experienced together. The sensation of fire, for example, is usually accompanied by the sensation of heat, so the two related ideas will be closely associated in our minds. Whenever we see a fire or think of one we think of it as hot. Similarly, we expect ice to be cold and un-

39

supported objects to fall, simply because we have experienced these connections frequently in the past. Some connections between sensations and ideas are natural, in that they depend on the nature of the physical world. Fire and heat, solidity and weight, are natural associations and such connections constitute 'scientific' knowledge. Other associations are artificial in that they depend on human choice and decision, and so constitute 'moral' knowledge. The association between the ideas of 'stealing' and 'punishment' is not a natural association. Society decides to punish thieves; no-one decides that fires should be hot. It was also a part of the doctrine that associations tend to be strengthened when they involve pleasurable consequences to the individual, for example, the association between the idea of virtuous conduct and the idea of a reward. Mill accepted this doctrine more or less in full, so that for him knowledge was simply a matter of having those associations of ideas which corresponded to the natural and artificial facts of the world, or, more strictly, to the order of the sensations we may have.

Education on this view is nothing more than the forming in the pupil's mind certain desirable trains of ideas, by presenting him with certain sequences of sensations. The associations required will be those which form the basis of the desired kind of behaviour, those which constitute the knowledge and attitudes most likely to produce happiness for the pupil and for others. The Utilitarian curriculum, not given in detail in the essay, would provide for associations of the natural kind, knowledge of the physical world and the behaviour of other people. This would enable the pupil to make correct predictions about the future course of events and to act accordingly. It would provide also for associations of the artificial sort, giving knowledge about how one ought to behave, the basis of generous, prudent, and equitable actions. It would include, presumably, the disciplines of science and mathematics, history and geography, and 'moral' subjects like literature, philosophy and religion. Possessing this knowledge the pupil would be able to act in a rational way, based on a correct appreciation of his situation. But merely being in possession of the right associations of ideas will not of itself produce the desired conduct. This must come from moral training and persuasion. Mill assumes that the pupil will only act to promote his own happiness, so he must be taught to associate his own happiness with that of others. Mill calls this 'social education'. It takes the form of associating the idea of social approval with the desired behaviour and disapproval with behaviour to be discouraged. These forces, by acting on the individual's desire for happiness and the avoidance of pain would, Mill thinks, be well nigh irresistible in moulding character in the desired way.

Mill does not give any detailed pedagogical recommendations in the essay, holding that to do so was impracticable in a brief article. We could, however, infer from his psychology what his assumptions about methods would be. The psychological assumptions were that if two sensations or ideas are joined frequently in experience the occurrence of one of them will tend to be accompanied or followed by the other. The most effective methods then would be those that secured the systematic joining of certain sensations and ideas in the pupil, by presenting him with those conjunctions frequently and making their establishment in his mind a source of satisfaction to him. Mill in fact used such methods in the education of his own children. In practice this could easily result in a regime of drilling and rote-learning, but from what we know of Mill's own teaching this was not so in his case. John Stuart Mill, who was educated by his father along strict utilitarian lines, admits that whatever else might be said of his education it was never a mere cramming. (26) James Mill tried to ensure that associations made in his pupil's mind were accompanied by some degree of understanding. He aimed at sagacity as well as at knowledge.

Mill's educational theory, then, in short, is this: Granted the need to produce an individual who, notwithstanding his natural egoism, is to be a means to the general happiness, then, by an appropriate arrangement of his experiences, associate in his mind those ideas which are the basis of desirable actions. Such associations will constitute the knowledge, the skills and the attitudes which will enable him to take his place in social life. The pressure of social approval or disapproval, by increasing or decreasing his own happiness, will prompt him to play his part well.

The Utilitarian theory is undeniably authoritarian in character. There is hardly anything in Mill corresponding to that interpretation of Rousseau which holds that the teacher is to be a mainly negative influence, simply providing the right environment for the child's development. The Utilitarians considered the acquisition of knowledge and the ability to use it so important for the wellbeing of mankind that they were prepared if necessary to force it on to the pupil. Intellectual training was as important as, indeed a part of, character training. There is little concern in Mill for what the pupil might be interested in, for his spontaneous impulses. It is his interest as a social being which is paramount, his interest as a free, responsible, moral member of an individualistic society. What he happens to be interested in as a child is of secondary importance. Utilitarian educational theory was subject-centred and teacher-centred, a traditional model. Mill and the Utilitarians generally were radicals in politics but they were not 'progressives' in education, as Rousseau might properly be said to be. In another respect too, their views may be contrasted with the popular interpretation of Rousseau. For the Utilitarians, except for the proviso that associations of ideas should follow the natural order of events, education was not to be 'according to nature'. Indeed, it was to prevail in spite of nature, certainly in spite of child nature. It was to be social, artificial and adult-centred.

v The educational theory of John Dewey

Plato and Mill may be regarded as the advocates of an authoritarian, subject-dominated education. John Dewey, by contrast, belongs with Rousseau on the progressive side, and his educational theory may, with some reservations, be thought of as a more or less modern version of Rousseau's, rendered in a transatlantic idiom.

Dewey wrote a great deal on education and his educational theory is to be found in a number of his works. The most comprehensive of his educational writings is *Democracy and Education* (1916). (10) What follows here is not a summary of any particular book but a general account of Dewey's position in education.

Dewey grew up in the second half of the nineteenth century in an America which was set to become one of the world's great industrial powers, and he lived to see America reach its twentieth-century stature. The America of his early manhood and early writing was however still the America of the developing frontier and his thinking was influenced by this fact. In such a society the ideal type of individual tends to be the self-reliant, resourceful, energetic pioneer, able to cope adequately in a world of pressing problems, solution of which is a condition of survival. What a predominantly frontier-type society needs is not scholars so much as practical men, able to turn their hands to a variety of tasks, to farming, to small-scale industry, to running a railway, a newspaper or a township. A young society like this is likely to place great store on enterprise, on individuality, on independence, and to be impatient with claims to privilege not based on merit and ability. Something of this attitude is revealed in Dewey's work. His initial assumption of value, as an educator, concerns the desirability of what might be called 'democratic man', the folk-hero of nineteenth-century American society, and now the 'common man' of our time. For Dewey the Platonic Guardian, the cultivated Émile and the Utilitarian bourgeois figure merge into something like the knowledgeable, self-reliant New England farmer or the handy factory operative in Detroit. The task of education is not the making of an aristocratic ruler, or a scholar, or even a middle class man, but modern man, urban democratic man.

Dewey's assumptions about the nature of man as the raw material of education disclose a wholly secular outlook. As a young man he was influenced by the work of Darwin, whose *Origin of Species* was published in 1859, the year Dewey was born. Like Darwin, Dewey saw man as essentially a part of the world of nature. Few philosophers have thought of man in less spiritual or mystical terms. For Dewey the material world is the sole sphere of man's activities. It is a world which has to be mastered and made to yield objects for human satisfaction, not merely as a condition of man's living well, but of his living at all. (10, Ch. 1) Man's life is a succession of urgent here-and-now problems to be solved. In the course of solving them and of mastering his environment, man acquires intelligence which for Dewey is simply another name for the habit of using one's mind effectively, with forethought and resourcefulness. Dewey assumes, then, that man is an active, social, problem-solving animal, for whom success in life is the continual mastery of his environment, the solution of problems about the provision of food, shelter, clothing, as well as those about social and political organisation. It would be wrong to suppose that he saw men as solely concerned with the gross material aspects of existence. Certainly, he regarded these things as basic, but he was well aware that there is more to living than this, and that when man's basic needs have been met his problems are secondary and derivative, arising from activities involving the arts and social life as such. None the less, Dewey's point is that man is a creature of this world, and that at whatever level of sophistication his life is lived, it is a matter of coping with problems, whether in the business of cooking or in the making of lyric poetry.

Dewey's assumptions about children follow from his view of man in general. Essentially children are active, exploring, problem-solving creatures. Dewey divides the child's life, roughly, into three stages of development, a 'play' period characterised by spontaneous activity of a fairly uncritical kind, a 'techniques' period in which the child learns to distinguish means and ends and to follow simple procedures, and lastly, a period of 'reflective attention' in which a more critical approach to problem-solving is possible. The emphasis throughout is on activity, which becomes more differentiated and purposeful as the child grows older. (9b, Ch. 4)

As with the other theories we have looked at we can distinguish between what is declared in Dewey's theory of education and what is undeclared and implied. The tacit assumption of value is the making of a certain type of individual, capable of living well in a certain sort of society, a democracy. As Dewey presents the theory, however, the declared aims involve a distinction between two sorts of experiences, between those which are 'educative' and those which are not, or, as Dewey puts it, between those which lead on to, or constitute, 'growth' and those which do not. (10, Ch. 4) This point, made in more than one of Dewey's educational writings, needs to be explained more fully.

What Dewey means is something like this: The individual lives in a world which presents him with a continuous succession of experiences. These experiences differ in respect of their consequences for the individual. Some are such as lead on to further experiences of a wider kind, which in turn lead on to yet further such experiences, with an indefinite widening of horizons. Such experiences, Dewey says, constitute 'growth' for the individual. They satisfy what he calls the criterion of 'continuity', that is, they involve a continual exponential enhancing of the quality of life. They are life-enriching. Other experiences are narrowing, in that they tend to restrict one's horizons, reducing the possibility of enhancing experiences in the future, and so do not lead on to, or constitute, personal growth. An example of an experience which would constitute growth would be a child's learning to read. Learning to read involves an interaction with one's environment, the tackling and solving of a number of problems, solution of which makes possible further experience of a widening kind, an initiation into literature, history and science, for example. These in turn broaden out, with new problems to solve and new forms of awareness, new opportunities of personal response. By contrast, activities like, say, playing darts or doing jigsaw puzzles, do not generally lead on to much beyond themselves and so do not widen one's horizons to any great extent, and so do not, in Dewey's sense, lead on to, or constitute, growth. Growth, for Dewey, involves the extension and development of one's powers and possibilities as a human being, and for him continued growth is synonymous with successful living.

Dewey usually identifies 'education' with 'growth' and sees it as a process of continuous interaction between the individual and his environment, going on throughout life, and not to be thought of simply in terms of formal schooling. This identification of education with personal growth inhibits him from admitting any external end to be served by education, the production of wealth, for example. In so far as men's activities produce goods and satisfactions they do so in a way which can be, and ought to be, constitutive of growth. So Dewey is reluctant to admit that education has, or can have, any aims beyond itself. The end of education is simply more education, more growth, or, as it is sometimes put, the aims of education are internal and intrinsic. This however is not inconsistent with Dewey's more or less undeclared aim, of producing a certain type of individual, a democratic, secular, technological man. This is simply the way in which 'growth' presents itself in the early twentieth century.

Although Dewey does not restrict education to formal schooling he is none the less concerned with education in its institutional sense, and with this in mind we can look at his assumptions about knowledge and pedagogical methods. His main assumption about knowledge is that it is essentially secular, about the way the world is, and that it is important in so far as it provides the basis for the problem-solving and the enhancement of life which constitutes individual growth. Dewey's general philosophical position is usually known as 'instrumentalism' or pragmatism, the root idea of which is that what counts as knowledge and truth is what works, what produces satisfactory results for men in their interaction with their environment. It would be an oversimplification, but not a very misleading one, to say that for Dewey knowledge is primarily scientific knowledge, awareness of the true nature of the world. This is the only kind of knowledge worth having, perhaps the only kind possible.

Dewey's assumptions about educational methods constitute a central part of his theory and give rise to some distinctive recommendations for pedagogy. He recognises that an important part of the education of children will take place in school but he is opposed to thinking of school as a place deliberately set apart from the rest of social life, a place where children are segregated and prepared for adult life. To think of schools in this way would be to divorce education from the real business of life, which is living, and so would defeat the purpose of education, which is individual growth. So Dewey recommends that the school should resemble, and be integrated with, the great society of which it is properly a part. The assumption here is that what happens in school is only justified in so far as it is a simplified and purified version of life outside the school. (10, Ch. 2) So there should be opportunities for activity by the children there, activities of the problem-solving sort, involving the acquisition and development of intelligence. Moreover the problems should be real problems, problems appropriate to the developmental stage reached by the child and which spring from his interests as a child, not adult problems suggested by his teachers, and not problems of the merely academic kind. The 'problems' to be found in a conventional mathematical textbook, for example, are not the kind which present themselves as problems to children. The child's problems will arise naturally from his needs, his need to understand what is going on in the world about him, his need to cope with this world, to *do* things for himself. The social life of a community is a rich complex of activities which the child is heir to; the business of the school

45

is to present him with a version of this world in such a way that he can, at his own level, take an active part in it. Here we have an assumption which links Dewey very closely with Rousseau, that the most effective educational methods are those which involve direct, first-hand experience and practical activity by the pupils, activity in which the need for knowledge and skill and the exercise of intelligence will make itself felt. In this way children will acquire knowledge and skills as a by-product of doing something else, finding out about something, making something, involving themselves in some practical enterprise. Dewey's criticism of the schools of his time was that the emphasis was always on the subject matter to be learned, on the textbook, or the teacher's words, whereas, he thought, it should be on the participatory activity of the pupil. So, the methods recommended by Dewey involved the children in working on topics which interested them, which presented real problems to them, which linked their activities to the life of the world outside the school, and which offered them those experiences which constitute growth. Children, he thought, should be encouraged to work together, as adults do, collaborating in various activities, making things, cooking, writing a magazine and so on. In this way they would come to face the human problems involved in working co-operatively and learn the 'democratic' virtues of tolerance, discipline, and social responsibility. These recommendations are 'child-centred', illustrative of what Dewey called the 'Copernican Revolution' in education: that henceforth the centre of the educational system was to be the child and not the subject matter or the teacher. The teacher's role was to be that of providing an environment in which children could work on their own, the teacher co-operating with them when necessary, helping them, advising them, but not imposing his views on them. Teaching, on this view, is not so much a matter of filling children up with ideas or knowledge as enabling them to acquire intelligence and skill by coping, under sympathetic guidance, with the world about them and the practical problems it provides. (9a and 9b) (10, Ch. 14)

Dewey's educational theory may be summarised as follows: Man is essentially an active, problem-solving creature. Ideally he is a developing, 'growing', socially conscious creature. To produce this ideal type the child must be set tasks which develop his intelligence, his capacity to live adequately, and this must be done in a way which makes him a co-operative social being. This calls for an education of the 'progressive', child-centred kind, making use of man's social resources to encourage individual growth.

vi Conclusion

The general theories of education outlined in this chapter cover the period between Greek times and the present day. As one might expect they differ in important ways. A theory which satisfied a Greek aristocrat of the fifth century BC is likely to be different from one which reflects the views of a man of the eighteenth century, or those of a modern American democrat like Dewey. But despite the differences there are some similarities, which this chapter has tried to bring out. Plato and Mill, for example, agree in giving what has been called the traditional or subject-centred model in education, where the main emphasis is placed on the importance of knowledge as a means of realising desirable social and individual ends. Rousseau and Dewey agree in giving the other side of the picture, the child-centred model, where the emphasis lies, not so much on the importance of knowledge as on individual activity and the need for first-hand participation by the pupil in the educational enterprise. The distinction between these two outlooks should not be exaggerated. The traditionalists, in Plato's day and now, also concern themselves with individual development, and the child-centred theorists in no way deny the importance of knowledge. The differences between these two points of view are very often simply differences of emphasis.

Then, underlying all four theories, and irrespective of differences in emphasis and in social and political outlook, there is a common structure. All see education as a means to an end, although the ends are differently formulated. All make assumptions about human nature, although the assumptions they make are not the same. All make the assumption that the pedagogy they prescribe is appropriate to the end they wish to realise. In each case there is a prescriptive means-ends model, of the form: Since men are like this, then, if you want to achieve a given end, a 'just' man, a 'natural' man, a 'modern' man, you must organise your educational arrangements in such-and-such a way. Each individual theory spells out the details of the model. It is, of course, open to anyone to discern in them one other similarity, that each involves a persuasive attempt to secure acceptance, not only of pedagogical recommendations, but of the social aims written into or implied in the theory. As was said at the beginning of this chapter, educational theory may serve as propaganda as well as backing for educational practice, and in reading educational writings this possibility should be kept in mind.

4

A critique of the historical theories

i *Introduction*

When we were dealing with the nature of scientific theories we said that their validity depended primarily on the facts of the observable world. Scientists look for empirical evidence which contradicts their conclusions, since it is the failure to find any such evidence which warrants their holding a scientific theory to be provisionally established. Educational theories do not stand or fall simply by the kind of evidence which would be crucial to a descriptive theory. A practical theory might well be open to criticisms based on empirical evidence but there are other ways in which it may be vulnerable. In this chapter we look at the general theories already outlined to see how and to what extent they might be criticised, and it will be useful to recapitulate here what was said earlier concerning the forms such criticism might take.

Each of these theories made certain assumptions, about aims, about human nature and about knowledge and methods. Assumptions about human nature might, undoubtedly, be criticised by an appeal to empirical evidence, to what had been established by psychologists or sociologists, and any educational theory based on assumptions which ran counter to such evidence could thus be shown to be inadequate. It might also be possible to argue that the assumptions in question could not be shown to be either true or false, that they were 'metaphysical' in character, untestable in principle. This too would cast doubts on the acceptability of the theory as a theory.

Assumptions about aims and objectives are open to attack in much the same way. Of course, we can't show educational aims to be objectionable simply because there are facts in the world which run counter to them. If our aim is to establish a democratic way of life, or saintliness in men, the *aim* is not damaged by evidence that many men aren't democrats or saints. This would merely show that the aim hadn't been realised, not that it was an aim to be rejected or that the theory which assumed it was invalid. But if the aim ran counter to the facts in that the facts made it impossible to realise the aim, then both the aim and the theory could be rejected as unrealistic. A theory might also be rejected on the grounds that it was impossible to show whether or not its aim had ever been realised. So too, any educational aim which rested on a philosophical position which was not itself open to substantial challenge, would be vulnerable because it would share the weakness of its philosophical support. Again, a theory might be criticised by showing that its aims were morally objectionable.

It might be possible to object to a theory in respect of its assumptions about the nature of knowledge. It might be shown, for instance, that these assumptions were incorrect or misleading in that they over-emphasised the importance of one sort of knowledge as compared with another. Assumptions about the general effectiveness of methods could be shown to be false, and here again scientific evidence would be relevant. Or it might be shown that although the methods recommended were effective they were none the less morally unacceptable, as hypnosis might be, and torture almost certainly would be. Lastly, it might be possible to show that there was no way of deciding whether the methods recommended could, or could not, achieve the desired end, that the assumptions about methods were untestable in principle.

It is hardly likely that all these criticisms would apply to the theories we are dealing with, but we shall find that some of them do, and that each of the theories is to some extent inadequate. It will be maintained however that the criticisms levelled at them do not require them to be rejected altogether, and that in spite of their shortcomings they still have something to offer.

ii Assumptions about aims

We could begin by examining the assumptions made in each case about educational aims. For Plato the declared aim was the realisation of a just state and men who could be citizens of such a state. The undeclared aim involved the education of a non-democratic élite, whose special claim was that its members were those most fitted to govern. The implication was that only this gifted minority could be brought to an appreciation of the ideal world of Forms, apprehension of which enabled one to know how to govern well. Plato's educational aim, then, was the production of wise and good rulers whose wisdom and goodness derived from this special grasp of reality which Plato calls knowledge, as opposed to opinion. Now, this aim rests upon assumptions of a recondite philosophical kind, namely, that the two-world account of reality is correct, that there *is* a world of Forms to be known, and whose apprehension enables or determines the Guardians to rule well. Plato of course provides arguments to support his doctrine of Forms. These arguments are complicated and technical and will not be reproduced here, but it can be said of them that they are not always good arguments. (see 14, Pt 1, Ch. 2) And the arguments are all the evidence we have. The Forms are supposed to exist outside both space and time, and are not amenable to scientific investigation. Thus the acceptance of the Platonic position in education depends largely on the degree of conviction his philosophical arguments produce, and his educational theory could be criticised on the ground that its aims rest upon metaphysical presuppositions not at all well established and perhaps not capable of being established, one way or the other. There may be an ideal world of Forms to be known, but the conclusion that there is rests on arguments which owe nothing to anything beyond themselves. Plato's educational aims, then, rely on a philosophical position of a metaphysical kind, and are vulnerable to the extent to which the philosophical position is vulnerable.

It could also be said that Plato's use of terms like 'just' and 'justice' is highly persuasive and question-begging. No-one wants to be unjust or against 'justice' so we are predisposed in favour of a theory which recommends action to secure a just society and just men. But we find that adherence to Plato's theory involves assent to a kind of society which we might otherwise want to stigmatise as inegalitarian, authoritarian and unfair. It could be argued that Plato's *Republic* is a blue-print for a class-society of workers and rulers, based on what Plato considers to be ineluctable differences between men. Here again, Plato presents his case with the advantages of genius, but whether one is convinced by him or not will depend on the significance one is prepared to give to a term like 'justice' and the extent to which one thinks a society based on differences in men, and a need for disciplined social stratification, is more desirable than one committed to individual freedom, equality and democracy. It might be thought that Plato's assumptions about ends are morally as well as philosophically debatable. (37)

Criticisms like this are, of course, themselves open to challenge. A Platonist could retort that the aim of wisdom and statecraft for the Guardians involved the development of reason, which is not merely a metaphysical matter. Moreover, it could be said that Plato was concerned, above all, with the common good and that his various recommendations aim at social harmony and order, the indispensable conditions for the happiness and well-being of all the citizens in the state whatever their roles. These points will not be developed here. Enough has been said to show some of the ways in which Plato's assumptions about ends might be criticised. Whether this criticism is justified or not is also a matter for debate.

Rousseau's theory suffers in that his overall aim is exasperatingly vague and that various interpretations of it are possible. He advocates an 'education according to nature' and his declared aim is sometimes given as the 'natural man'. When we try to grasp what this means, however, we are in some difficulty. According to one interpretation Rousseau sees 'natural man' as man in a pre-social state of nature, unspoiled by civilisation. Yet this natural man has somehow to live in an imperfect social order. How this is possible is by no means clear and thus understood Rousseau's aim seems confused or confusing. On another interpretation 'natural' man is ideal man, man as he might be, his nature realised to the full. This view rests on Rousseau's assumption that man is a perfectible being. The notion of perfectibility is not very precise. Rousseau certainly says in the *Discourse on the Origin of Inequality*, that man's capacity for improving himself is almost unlimited, so it is possible to interpret him as implying elsewhere, in the *Émile* for example, that the natural man is man improved more or less indefinitely. Such a thesis has its drawbacks, however. All we can discover about actual men is that they are, generally, improvable. To say that they are indefinitely improvable, or perfectible almost without limits, may be to assert what is questionable or perhaps untestable. It is difficult to know what evidence would settle this point. Perhaps a more defensible interpretation of Rousseau's position is that, for him, natural man is man developed to the full extent of his present powers, whatever they are. 'Nature' would be understood here in the Aristotelean sense of 'what a thing is in its perfection' and natural man as perfected man, improved to his limits as a human being. Rousseau no doubt meant something like this, although it must be said that his overall aim is somewhat lacking in clarity.

James Mill's assumption about ends was that it is the business of education to prepare individuals for the promotion of the greatest amount of happiness for the greatest number of people. This was the whole point of getting pupils to acquire knowledge and skills—these things were the means by which the pupil could be a source of happiness, to himself and to others. There seems to be a good deal of sense in this, but however attractive the principle of utility may be, it must be recognised that it is an assumption none the less, and that there seems to be no rational way of convincing anyone who denies its adequacy that it should be adopted. Mill seems to have thought it self-evidently true, such that no rational man could doubt it, but it is not so. It is quite possible to claim that there are more important things than happiness, justice, for example, or integrity. So we might properly ask why happiness should be the end proposed and not these other virtues. Mill would no doubt reply that other virtues are so only because they conduce to human happiness, but this point is arguable. We might think that, say, justice was supremely important, even though it produced less than the greatest amount of happiness. Mill's assumption, then, that happiness is, or ought to be, the end for all rational activity, is, in a sense, unsupported. As an ultimate moral principle no further reasons can be given why anyone should adopt it in preference to other ends. This is not to say that as an assumption it must be rejected but merely that a practical theory grounded upon it has to face this kind of criticism. It is only fair to say that this point holds against all assumptions as to ultimate matters of value, Plato's, Rousseau's and Dewey's, no less than Mill's.

Dewey assumes the end of education to be individual growth, the ideal of a personality forever extending its horizons in experience. A criticism of this notion of growth as an end is that it is confusing and to some extent misleading. When we think of growth in the ordinary way we may think of it as a natural process, perhaps of a biological kind, something that goes on in the world more or less independently of human decision. Plants and animals, even children, 'grow' in this biological sense, with or without our help. But this 'natural' sense of growth is descriptive in character, and is neutral with respect to ends. Things can grow towards good or towards evil. So we can generally ask, 'Growth towards what?', meaning the end to which the process points and which can be evaluated. Dewey does not take quite this view of growth. For him growth involves having experiences, but he will only count as growth those experiences which have a widening, life-enhancing effect on the individuals concerned. He holds some experiences to be educative and some not. So 'growth' is not simply having experiences, or more experiences, but having more experiences of a certain kind, those judged to be valuable. But this would seem to impart into the notion of growth itself a value element not usually found there. Growth is not now *towards* some end which may be seen as valuable, but itself involves a valuable end. It is for this reason that Dewey is able to say that education has no ends or values beyond itself, education simply is growth. There is nothing objectionable in this so long as it is recognised that when

Dewey speaks of growth he is not merely referring to some natural process, and that growth involves decisions of value on someone's part. This point could be made in respect of all who, like Rousseau, Froebel and Dewey, offer a 'growth' model of education, and particularly where, as with Froebel, the idea of growth is given in quasi-natural terms, on the analogy of plants and flowers, and used to support recommendations that the child, like the plant, must be allowed to do its own growing without too much help or interference by the teacher. In fact, the notion of growth in educa-tion, if it is to be valuable at all, involves considerable intervention by the teacher, who must make sure that the child's actual experi-ences in school do amount to growth. This, however, presupposes a commitment to some scale of values as to what experiences are worthwhile, and may be thought to raise for Dewey an unanswered question about the basis of this value commitment. One could ask: 'Why are experiences of this sort considered to be valuable?' To say that it is because they constitute growth would seem to be arguing in a circle. (8, Ch. 3)

This whole matter of fundamental principles, aims and ends, is complicated and controversial and nothing more has been attempted here than to show how criticisms might be made at this level. The writers we have been discussing are open to various kinds of criticism in respect of their assumptions about ends in education. Sometimes, as did Plato, they try to support an overall position by appeals to metaphysical arguments which may not carry con-viction. Sometimes, as with Rousseau, they are not altogether clear about what their educational aims are, or involve. Where, as in the case of Mill, their aims are fairly clear, they may rest them on principles which are not self-evidently true, though they may be thought to be so. Lastly, as with Dewey, the overall aim may be given in a misleading way, where what is in fact a prescription involving a judgment of value, is given in terms like 'growth', more appropriate to the description of a natural process. Criticisms like this are not meant to be wholly negative. They serve to make the point that to be adequate an overall educational aim must not only be clear and unambiguous, but must rest on normative principles recognised for what they are, deliberate decisions about what is to count as valuable. Such decisions are always open to challenge and it may well be that ultimate positions of value are not capable of rational support. This does not mean, however, that our value judgments at lower levels, at the level of educational aims, for example, need lack objectivity. Value judgments are made objective by our ability to give good reasons to support them.

iii *Assumptions about human nature*

We can now turn to the assumptions made about human nature. Plato, as we said in Chapter 3, thought of human beings as composed of a body and a soul. He is not always clear about the nature of a soul, but he thinks of it, generally, as an incorporeal existent which accompanies the body and influences it, but is separable from it. The soul was thought to have existed before the body and at least one aspect of the soul, the rational part, exists after the death of the body and is immortal. (36) It is, however, part of Plato's case that individual souls are not all of the same kind. Some he likens to gold and silver, others to copper and iron. The temporal joining of soul and body Plato regards as an inconvenience to the rational part of the soul, since the body and its demands hinder the soul's rational activity. The body belongs to the world of appearances, whereas the rational element in the soul belongs to the world of Forms, where it began. It is this rational aspect of the soul, the seat of reason, which must, by education, be directed away from a concern with bodily matters, back towards the world of reality. For Plato education is essentially the nurture of the soul and this is especially important for those with the potentiality for development which Plato alludes to when he speaks of those with gold and silver in their souls. The lower orders of society, whose souls are predominantly appetitive, are merely to be trained in crafts and techniques designed to meet appetitive needs. Those who are to be Guardians, however, emerge as philosophers, and for them the nurture of the soul involves the development of the rational part, becoming directly acquainted with the world of Forms and the knowledge required for the wise ruling of the state.

A possible criticism of this approach and of the assumptions it involves is one similar to that levelled against Plato's assumptions about aims. Plato's account of the soul contains metaphysical and mystical elements, holding, for example, that one aspect of the soul is immortal and has had experience of the world of Forms prior to its taking possession of the body. This leads him to maintain in other dialogues, the *Phaedo* (36) and the *Meno* (35) for example, that learning is really a 'remembering' of what the soul once knew and had forgotten. This whole account is such that there seems to be no way of finding out for certain whether it is true or not. We have no other warrant for it than the arguments Plato uses, in *The Republic* and elsewhere, to establish his position and these are often inconclusive and sometimes fallacious. Whether a man has a soul, in Plato's sense, or not, and what sort of thing the soul might be, and whether or not *this* is what education has to do with, are matters of debate, where the arguments are seldom more than persuasive and where there is nothing but the argument to guide us. If we ignore the metaphysical aspects of Plato's case and see him as simply making general psychological observations about men—that men are different in temperament and character, and recommending that the more rational shall be the rulers, the bravest the soldiers and the rest the producers—there may be a good deal in what he says. Whether in doing this we should be understanding Plato as he intended he should be understood is another matter.

Rousseau and James Mill were both men of the eighteenth century and though very different in temperament and character they shared many of the intellectual presuppositions of their time. Nevertheless there are differences as well as similarities in their assumptions about human nature.

Rousseau holds that the individual is essentially a 'developing' creature and that the child's development as a child must be taken into account in educating him. Education must be according to his 'nature', which Rousseau often seems to equate with biological growth. Rousseau has also a doctrine of development stages, in which the child is supposed to recapitulate the history of the human race, the infant corresponding to the animal stage, the boy to the savage stage, and so on, but perhaps his most controversial assumption about children, and one which will be dealt with here, is that they are 'naturally good'. Everything, he says, is good as it leaves the hand of God. The implication here is that things which begin well may deteriorate through misuse, and this is true, he thinks, of men. Men may be, indeed are, corrupted by society. In society men learn how to be insincere, selfish, cunning and vain. So it is society which is to be blamed for the ills of mankind, and this assumption enters his theory as a reason for rejecting society, or seeming to do so, as a means of educating Émile. Émile is to be kept away, as a child, from the society which would corrupt his original goodness. But what are we to say of such an assumption? Only, as we said in Chapter 2 in respect of a similar view held by Froebel, that there seems to be no way of establishing its truth or falsity. Rousseau seems to be offering it as an empirical generalisation about children, but if this were so there must be at least the possibility of evidence to show it to be false. It is, however, difficult to see how any empirical evidence could do this. If a child brought up in society turns out to be a bad man this would support Rousseau's view that children can be corrupted by society : if he turns out a good man this supports the view that he was good naturally and from the beginning. So the assumption seems to hold whatever the evidence. But an assumption about human beings which can be maintained whatever the evidence is not a very promising basis for an educational theory, since it gives no real information at all. It is a dubious bit of metaphysics, disguised as an assertion of substance. Criticism of a similar kind could be raised against Rousseau's view that human nature is indefinitely perfectible.

James Mill did not share Rousseau's optimistic belief in the natural goodness of man, nor did he place any emphasis on the notion of 'growth', as Rousseau did, but he did incline to the Helvetian view that men are equally and indefinitely capable of improvement, by education, good government and sound social institutions. (6) This is the perfectibility thesis again, and in so far as Mill's educational theory embodies this conviction, it is open to the criticism that one of its assumptions about the nature of man is untestable and questionable.

One other important assumption about human beings held by both Rousseau and Mill was the empiricist view that the human mind is a kind of receptacle to be filled up with sensations and ideas. The mind, it was thought, works on these ideas, linking them together to form sequences, comparing them, contrasting them, recalling them, and in this way obtains a picture of the world which is the external source of these ideas. Education is a matter of giving the pupil the right combinations of ideas, those combinations which mirror the way the outside world operates, since this constitutes the basis for effective action. This view of the mind has been strongly criticised by later psychologists. The psychological model, assumed by Locke and accepted by Rousseau and Mill, involved the mind's apprehending particular experiences and piecing them together to make significant wholes out of parts. Knowledge, it was assumed, is made up of separate ideas linked together by association, as a wall is made out of individual bricks. Teaching was a matter of getting the pupil to make the desired associations of particular sensations and ideas. A later psychological tradition was to throw considerable doubt on the adequacy of this crude associationist view. The Gestalt psychologists claimed that the mind, so far from being the mere recipient of experiences to work upon, plays an active part in perception and cognition, striving to make sense of its various experiences by interpreting them in terms of meaningful wholes from the beginning. The contribution of the Gestalt psychologists to the theory of learning will be looked at again in the next chapter. At this point it can be said of both Rousseau and Mill that their psychological assumptions tend to be crude and naïve and need to be supplemented by more adequate knowledge of the way the human mind works.

An assumption about human nature which Mill and the Utilitarians held is that men do, and can, only act in such a way as they think will increase their own pleasure or diminish their own pain. This is the doctrine known as 'psychological hedonism'. Mill builds it into his educational theory when he recommends that the child must be taught always to seek his own happiness in that of others. The assumption is that he can only seek his own happiness : the recommendation is that he should find it only in making others happy. This doctrine is really damaging to Mill's theory, since it effectively withdraws all moral worth from actions. If men *can* only do what they think will make themselves happy, there is no point in saying that they *ought* to promote the happiness of others, where it conflicts with their own. At most they can be got to pursue the general happiness, but they can't be morally required to pursue it. It is unfortunate that Mill made this doctrine a part of his theory, since although it is plausible it is also erroneous. Its plausibility arises from a confusion. Whenever anyone acts he certainly does what he then most prefers to do. It would not be his action otherwise. So all actions are selfish in this tautological sense. But this doesn't prevent some actions from being, in a substantial sense, unselfish. It doesn't follow that when someone does what he wants to do he is simply aiming at his own pleasure. Men frequently set out deliberately to benefit others; that they get pleasure from doing so is incidental and doesn't make their actions any less unselfish. Psychological hedonism was not really essential to Mill's position. All he needed to assume for his purposes was that, although men do often act selfishly, they need not do so. They can be brought, in various ways, by example, by moral argument, as well as by reward and punishment, to seek the well-being of others. This would be quite consistent with what he maintains in the essay.

The assumptions made by both Rousseau and Mill, about the raw material of education, human nature, are thus open to criticism in the light of subsequent psychological knowledge and developments in philosophical analysis. Dewey, living much of his life in the twentieth century and having access to the results of studies not available to his predecessors, is not open to the same degree of criticism in respect of his own view of human nature. So far as it goes, Dewey's account of man as an experiencing, exploring, problem-solving, social being comes near to the truth of the matter. It may be objected, however, by some, that Dewey tends to over-stress the secular, materialistic aspects of human life, that he places too much emphasis on the importance of practical knowledge, and that he is somewhat lacking in his appreciation of the 'spiritual' aspects of human experience.

iv *Assumptions about knowledge and methods*

Assumptions about the effectiveness of methods will generally be derived from assumptions about the nature of knowledge, and about human nature. Plato grounds his mainly on his assumptions about knowledge. Plato, it will be remembered, saw knowledge as involving certainty, which came only from a grasp of the Forms. All else was opinion. The point of acquiring knowledge was that it would enable men to live well, to know what they ought to do and why. In particular it would enable the Guardians to rule the state wisely and keep it in moral health. The methods best calculated to facilitate grasp of this knowledge were those which turned men's attention away from the appearances of things, towards the true reality which lay behind appearances. In *The Republic* Plato recommends as effective and necessary for this higher education, mathematical studies followed by dialectic, a special sort of logic akin to mathematics.

The actual content and methods of this study are not given in any detail, and this makes criticism of it difficult. What follows is offered with some diffidence. It could be said that the effectiveness of any such methods would depend on the prior consideration whether the end to be achieved is possible. This would depend on the validity of Plato's metaphysics. If there is a world of Forms to be known, then the mathematical and logical regime hinted at by Plato may be the most effective way of getting to know it. But the metaphysical position does not command universal acceptance, and if it is not accepted, the programme of studies Plato recommends will not seem compelling either. It is a matter of some speculation whether the end Plato has in view is a possible one, and if it is, whether the methods recommended would in fact be effective. Quite apart from this a further criticism is possible. The point of the mathematical and dialectical studies was to give a grasp of the Forms, ultimately an understanding of the Form of the Good, which involved knowledge and certainty. Armed with this true knowledge the Guardians would be able to apply it to the affairs of the state, and rule well. The implication is that in knowing the Form of the Good one grasps a fundamental principle from which may be derived, not only theoretical truths like the laws of nature and the principles of mathematics—which hitherto have, according to Plato, been grasped only as hypotheses—but also important principles of practice, guides for action, all of which carry the certainty which belongs to the fundamental principle. Two difficulties arise from this. First, it is hard to see what the *content* of any such fundamental principle could possibly be. What fundamental truth could provide the Guardians with practical principles to meet all eventualities? Plato does not say, and the whole matter is left vague. Secondly, it could be argued that no principle about what ought to happen, or in fact does happen, in the world can have the certainty that Plato requires. The certainty Plato has in mind is the demonstrable certainty we associate with mathematics. Plato was a disciple of Pythagoras and like the Pythagoreans he seems to have thought that the world of appearances was one which had underlying mathematical properties, an order which, once the laws of mathematics had been established, could be known with the same sort of certainty. But it may be questioned whether reality does have this mathematical ground plan and it can be argued that the certainty of mathematics and logic has no application to anything that goes on in the empirical world. The certainty we find in mathematics comes from our obeying the rules we build into the game. The conclusions of mathematics are necessarily true because we do not allow them to be otherwise, they follow from the meanings we give to the terms used. Thus we pay a price for the certainty of mathematics, namely that it gives us no substantial information about the empirical world. If, on the other hand, we apply mathematics to the empirical world it forfeits its demonstrable certainty. The role of mathematics here is to give precision to scientific thinking, but the precision of science is the precision of probability, not the precision of deductive logic. Mathematics fits the world well enough, but contingently so. Scientists have long since given up looking for demonstrable certainty about the world; the whole point of science is that its conclusions are hypothetical and may be false. What Plato seems to have wanted was the assurance which belongs to pure mathematics transferred somehow to the world of everyday life. Grasp of the Form of the Good, he thought, would give this double assurance. This seems doubtful. This scepticism does not deny the value of mathematics and logic in education; it merely questions the primacy Plato accords to them in his theory. Plato tends to exaggerate the role of mathematics as the basis of method. (14, Ch. 9)

The methods advocated by Rousseau are similar in some ways to those recommended later by Dewey, and it will be convenient to take them together for the purpose of critical comment. Rousseau in Book 2 of *Émile*, and Dewey in more than one of his educational writings, recommend that education should be, as we would now say, child-centred, that the child should not, generally, be told what he can be led to find out for himself, and that the emphasis should be on first-hand experience by the pupil, the child following his own interests and impulses. Both Rousseau and Dewey see the teacher as supervisory rather than as overtly didactic. Rousseau stresses the need to let the child learn only what he needs to learn as a child. Dewey advocates that such learning should take place in meaningful problem-situations which involve the acquisition of intelligence, and, he would add, in a social context where the child can learn from others. In both cases the assumptions about methods derive from a view about the nature of knowledge and the nature of children. For both Rousseau and Dewey knowledge is a means of personal development, towards the natural man, or towards individual growth, respectively, and for each the knowledge demanded is that which is significant for the child as such, not knowledge appropriate to the needs of the adult he may one day become. There is a good deal in this, and the point needs to be made. None the less, it is possible to raise some doubts about the general applicability of such methods. Rousseau's assumptions here may be seen, on one interpretation of his position, as anti-intellectual in character, stressing the active, exploratory, personality-development aspect of education rather than the initiation of the child, by those in possession, into the cultural heritage of books and formalised knowledge. This indeed may not be the best construction which can be placed on Rousseau's pedagogy, but Rousseau certainly lays himself open to such an interpretation. In so far as this approach is adopted in practice it might be criticised as tending towards 'soft' pedagogy and the lowering of educational standards. (3) Dewey's insistence on the active, co-operative, 'project-centred' learning situation might be criticised as time-consuming in practice and perhaps unnecessary for the more intelligent child. (2) Moreover, Dewey's recommendations presuppose a philosophical assumption about the nature of knowledge which is debatable. It could be argued that pragmatism does not give a tenable theory of knowledge and that the truth of a proposition and its usefulness are separate matters. This, if true, would not be decisive against Dewey's pedagogy as such, since active, practical, problem-solving activity might be valuable on other grounds than those sanctioned by pragmatism, but it would mean that these recommendations did not have the theoretical backing Dewey claimed for them.

Mill's pedagogy would need to rest on methods for getting the right association of ideas in the child's mind, those which supply the grounds for utilitarian behaviour. This would mean the reiteration of those trains of sensations and ideas which give a correct picture of the world and a correct notion of the probable consequences of actions. In the classroom it would involve activities which could easily degenerate into mere drilling and cramming. As indicated earlier, Mill himself did not allow this to happen in his own teaching, but it is a possibility implicit in the theory.

From what we know of Mill's practice, however, he is in no doubt that it is the teacher who is to set the pace and direction of the learning process. The teacher is there to present the material; the pupils task is to accommodate himself to the situation and to achieve the desired associations. Education is to be formal, teacher-centred or subject-centred. In practice Mill approved of the 'monitorial' system of instruction invented or popularised by Joseph Lancaster, and he used this essentially teacher-centred method for educating his own children.

A general objection to Mill's pedagogy derives from the crudeness of the psychology presupposed by it. Mill regarded the mind as something to be filled up with useful associations, and assumed that the pupil was to be stored with the knowledge required for the promotion of happiness. This makes the pupil a passive receiver of sensations, which runs counter to what is now believed about the working of the mind. There is little reason to suppose that the mind is merely a receptacle into which sensations may be poured, to be worked up into trains of ideas. The mind is, rather, an active, originating instrument, with structuring principles of its own. It selects experiences, it grasps experiences as wholes; it seeks insights. The view of the mind as a blank sheet for sensations to be imprinted on, or as a warehouse where ideas are stored, is now thought to be thoroughly misleading, and Mill's model of an educational situation, with its suggestion of 'filling up' by the teacher and receptivity by the pupil, seems crude and unimaginative if not positively wrong. The situation is more complicated and children are far more complicated than the empiricist model would allow. Again, Mill's emphasis on the importance of receiving knowledge, as distinct from active, self-expressive, initiatory experiencing by the pupil, gives his pedagogy a somewhat over-intellectualised air. If it is true that Rousseau underestimates the value of formalised knowledge, and there is some doubt about this, Mill may certainly be thought to have over-estimated it.

A philosophical objection which can be levelled at epistemologies of the 'sensationist' type, like Mill's, is that attempts to build up a knowledge of the world from private sensations are self-defeating. If knowledge is simply of our sensations and ideas, as is often held by those who offer such a view, it is difficult to see how we can ever have knowledge of the external world which is supposed to produce those sensations and ideas. Neither Locke nor Mill ever dealt satisfactorily with this difficulty.

v *The usefulness of the historical theories*

This chapter so far has been deliberately critical of the four theories outlined earlier. This is not meant to belittle the achievements of those who offered them. Despite their possible shortcomings in detail, the theories have considerable point and value. The criticisms have been introduced to indicate some of the ways theories of this kind may be called to account, to show that they can be called to account as educational theories. This is needed to rebut the charge that since they are not scientific theories there is no significant way in which they can be subjected to scrutiny. The claim made here is that so far as educational theories are concerned it is not the case that anything can be said or recommended with impunity. Theories of education make recommendations based partly on factual or supposedly factual assumptions, partly upon assumptions of value. These assumptions may always be questioned, by appeals to criteria of a scientific, moral, or philosophical kind, the various assumptions being amenable to criticisms in these different ways. It is because they can be so questioned that educational theories can claim to rank as theories. We may now make the further claim that the general theories we have dealt with survive the criticisms made against them and that whilst the criticisms may prevent their unqualified adoption for practice, they do not warrant their total rejection. As some of the historical general theories in science, the Ptolemaic theory or the Newtonian system, for example, retain their vitality because they still provide useful, if not accurate, ways of looking at the world, these historical general theories of education still have something valuable to offer. This claim we must now try to make good.

None of these traditional theories will do as they stand, as guides for current practice. They are all open to criticism in detail, and in one sense they may be said to be out-of-date. They are all products of their time and based on assumptions not always defensible and often different from those we would make today. They are often based on knowledge less complete than we now have at our disposal. It could then, be asked, why anyone other than a historian should bother about them? Why should we spend time in reading up Plato or Rousseau or even Dewey for our contemporary educational needs? One answer to this is that although they are historically dated, this is perhaps the least important aspect of them, and in one sense they are not out-of-date at all. Their relevance lies in the fact that they raise important matters of general interest which transcend the limitations imposed by their place in time. They are like windows through which we may look upon the educational scene. Each separate window looks out on a different aspect of the whole, each vantage point gives a different view and perspective. Each of the theories draws our attention to a feature of education which is important and which might be overlooked. Each theory is itself limited and incomplete, and usually in some respects erroneous, so each vantage point gives no more than a partial view. But each is useful in concentrating attention on some important part of the whole.

We do not, for example, have to adopt Plato's assumptions about the nature of reality or his élitist social philosophy, but we can understand him as drawing our attention to the fact that there is an order beneath the seeming chaos of experience, and that an exact and disciplined grasp of this order is a condition of a rational and civilised life. The order may not be of the kind that Plato thought it was, and we may not be able to come by a grasp of it by the methods Plato recommends, but that we need this grasp and understanding is an important truth, and one that ought not to be ignored. The search for order, for objective standards of excellence, for accuracy and discipline, is an indispensable part of a true education, and Plato's insistence on the importance of knowledge and understanding may be seen as underlining this point. Plato saw education as predominantly the development of reason, and although he took a more restricted view of reason than we might do today, when we think of 'reason' more in terms of 'good reasons', regard for evidence and impartiality, than as involving the apprehension of occult Forms, so far as his main point goes he may well be thought to be right. Reading Plato is a way of reminding ourselves on this point. Much the same can be said of Mill's contribution. Mill was a hard, rather unsympathetic character and his theory reflects his dryness and lack of humour, but he draws our attention to features of education which ought not to be overlooked. He emphasises the fact that a civilised life is only possible when men have the kind of knowledge that forms the basis of civilised behaviour, and the disposition to act on that knowledge. Mill was himself a highly cultivated man, and, like Plato, takes his stand on the fundamental importance of knowledge and understanding as the key to the good life; unlike Plato he sees this good life in terms of democratic procedures leading to the maximising of the public happiness. Plato and Mill both emphasise the role of the intellect in education, and in a world in which intellectualism is constantly under attack, this emphasis needs to be given.

Rousseau, by contrast, focuses attention on the nature of the individual who is to be taught. This was an aspect of the enterprise which the severely intellectualist approach of, say, James Mill, was apt to neglect. Rousseau's *Émile*, whilst not denying the importance of knowledge, urges us to see the child for what he is, not a miniature adult but a child, with a child-like life to live. This involves looking at education along another perspective, to give us a new insight into what is involved in it, an insight no teacher can afford to ignore. Rousseau insists that education must involve the consideration of childish interests and activities, with experience at first hand, and an awareness by teachers of the rich developmental life of the children they teach. It would be unfair to suggest that Rousseau is unique in this; Plato was not unmindful of the developmental history of children; but Rousseau makes the peculiar perfection of childhood central to his theory, in a way that Plato in *The Republic* does not. Dewey reinforces the Rousseau position, stressing the need to put the child at the centre of the educational enterprise and emphasising the personal growth aspect of it. He adds another view, namely that in a democratic society education must be significant for all its members, and this may involve broadening the notion of education beyond that which would have recommended itself to the essentially middle-class outlook of Rousseau and Mill. Dewey thus opens up another perspective, drawing attention to the need to enlist the interests and to capture the attention of those who, in a modern society, are to be educated but who will not generally involve themselves in an education of the scholarly and intellectualised kind appropriate to minds nurtured in the eighteenth century. Rousseau had the intelligent middle-class child mainly in mind and although Mill advocated education for the working class he tended to think of education in a way that would probably not have appealed greatly to the masses he proposed to benefit by it. Dewey, by contrast, is the educational theorist of the ordinary child, the child that most teachers spend their lives in teaching and in whom, Dewey admits, intellectual interest is not a dominant trait. (9b) Dewey calls attention to the needs, interests and purposes which the education of this child presupposes.

Understood in this way, these traditional general theories may be seen to be relevant and useful for present day practice. It is not suggested that any one of them should be adopted without qualification as a guide to practice, although many of the practical recommendations made in them can be used with effect. A better approach would be to consider each of them as giving useful insights into what goes on in schools and into what ought to be going on there. The teacher who knows something of what Plato and Mill, Rousseau and Dewey have to say, and, one might add, Froebel and Herbart, Pestalozzi and Spencer, is thereby better equipped to understand the various strands of policy and practice which are woven into educational life, since each of these theorists has contributed something to the present climate of opinion. Such a teacher is not only equipped to understand what is going on, but also to criticise and evaluate present trends in educational practice, to confront, for example, the often over-enthusiastic and unconscious disciples of Plato and Mill with correctives drawn from Rousseau or Dewey, and vice versa. The contemporary dialogue between the adherents of 'traditional' and 'progressive' ways of teaching may be thought of as an on-going debate between the theorists we have been discussing.

5

The groundwork of educational theory

i Introduction

The historical theories we have discussed may be useful in providing vantage points from which to view present educational issues and practice, but it may well be asked: 'And what now? What educational theory of a general kind is appropriate and relevant to our own time in the way that Rousseau's theory could be said to have been relevant to his?' The last major work in educational theory in English was Dewey's *Democracy and Education*, published in 1916. Our world, however, is very different from that of 1916 and some restatement of general theory might be thought to be due, if not overdue. Whether such a restatement is likely is a matter for speculation, but it is worth pointing out that general theories of the kind we have been discussing have nowadays gone out of fashion, together with large-scale theories in many other fields of study. Why this is so is not altogether clear, but it is at least partly due to the growth and complexity of modern knowledge. Knowledge has expanded prodigiously during the past half century and man's confidence in his ability to use this material to give comprehensive theories has declined. Scientists and philosophers alike now tend to restrict themselves to fairly limited areas of research. They have increasingly become specialists rather than global strategists in their subjects.

This is certainly true of educational studies. The twentieth century differs from the nineteenth and the eighteenth in that we now know so much more about the psychological and sociological aspects of education, about the way children grow, develop and behave, about the conditions under which learning takes place and about the most effective ways of teaching. It is very different from the situation in Rousseau's day, or Mill's, or even Dewey's. Rousseau did no large-scale studies, as modern child psychologists have done, to find out how children think and feel. His pedagogy owed more to intuition than to any extended practical experience or observation. He was more of an amateur of genius than a professional educationalist. The same may be said of James Mill. Mill gives the impression of having worked out his educational theory on the basis of a few unargued assumptions about human nature and human minds, without looking farther than his own library and, perhaps, his own children, and he seems to have had little real understanding even of them. Like Plato and like Rousseau he lacked knowledge of the facts about education. But this paucity of knowledge was something of an advantage to them as theorists. It was possible for them to handle all the available data and to present what seemed to them fairly complete and satisfactory theories. Present day educationalists, quite properly, lack their confidence. Educationalists nowadays are forced to be specialists, educational psychologists, sociologists of education, historians and philosophers of education, simply because the details of the whole field are too much for any one man to deal with. This does not prevent attempts at general theorising, but it tends to work against them.

Again, a general theory of education involves a commitment to values as ends, and we do not have nowadays the clear certainty about values some of our predecessors enjoyed. It is more difficult now to find an overall aim to take the place of aristocratic élitism or the 'natural man' or 'the Christian gentleman', aims which served well enough in the past. Even ends like 'the greatest happiness of the greatest number' and 'the common man' have their critics in educational circles, where often the implication of 'worse' is seen in the notion of 'more'. Thus the present uncertainty about values in western society inhibits rather than encourages attempts at overall theorising in education.

The question, then: 'What general theory of education is specifically relevant to our time?' is not easy to answer. In one sense it can be said that there is no such general theory. There is no contemporary version of *The Republic* or *Émile*. Yet it would be wrong to write off general theory altogether. The need for it remains. Teachers now, as in the past, need some general theoretical justification for what they do in their classrooms if their work is not to be aimless and incoherent. It is part of the purpose of this book to suggest that such theory is possible and, indeed, available. General theory of education is still on the agenda, but instead of being formulated and presented in a fairly compact way, as hitherto, it tends now to be available in a more piecemeal form. The increase in relevant knowledge has made a division of labour inevitable, and so, instead of finding theory given in completeness by some single

67

writer, we find the task taken on by different individuals, each contributing to the end in a specialised way. Educational theory is thus less tidy, more fragmented, than it once was. The picture has now to be put together out of its parts, the summarised conclusions of the specialists who work in different areas of enquiry, and the commitment to values which will make those specialist conclusions relevant. In short, the teacher must be his own general theorist of education. This does not mean that he must assume the impossible task of mastering all the details of the knowledge available. It means that he must be prepared to draw upon the broad conclusions of those who have done the detailed and specialised work, and to use those conclusions for his own ends in education, whatever they may be.

In this chapter we shall approach the making of a contemporary theory of education by looking first at some of these specialist contributions, those of the psychologists and the sociologists of education. These contributions may be regarded as providing us with assumptions which are, more or less, up-to-date and, so far as they go, accurate, and as such forming a reliable basis for educational prescriptions. Two points might be made here. First, in the space available only some of the most significant contributions may be dealt with. It is not suggested that the contributions mentioned are the only important ones in this field. Second, the findings will themselves be theories, and they may be theories of different logical types. Some will be straightforwardly descriptive, scientific theories based on experimental procedures and evidence. Others will be less straightforward, sometimes themselves involving assumptions not wholly amenable to scientific checking. Ideally, perhaps it would be better to exclude all contributory theories which do not qualify in the straightforward, scientific sense, but to do so would exclude at least one contribution of considerable educational interest. To meet this difficulty, whenever a contributory theory may be thought to lack scientific rigour, this will be pointed out.

ii Child study

The contributions made by the psychologists will be dealt with under two broad headings. The first will include the work of some of those who have something important to say about child development. The second will deal with the findings of those who have been mainly concerned with the technicalities of learning. These two fields of study cannot, strictly, be separated, since one aspect of a child's development will involve the fact of his learning; but we may make a rough division here for our purpose. We will begin with an outline of some findings in child development.

One set of assumptions basic to any general theory of education concerns the nature of children as such. The historical theorists made assumptions of this kind which often derived hardly at all from any detailed study of children. Often the assumptions depended on a religious or metaphysical position: children were assumed to be naturally good, or bad, or perfectible, or to develop according to some pre-ordained pattern. Such assumptions were usually quite untestable, and the theories which depended upon them were weakened by this fact. In modern times, however, psychologists and others have set out to discover what children really are like, how they grow and develop, and a whole new field of study, child psychology and child study, has grown up. The child psychologist studies children, as any other scientist studies his material, as objectively as possible, by observation and by experiment. What was often the subject of mere conjecture has been subjected to disciplined scrutiny by those who are not concerned with myths or anecdotes about children but with hard facts about them. Child psychologists have instituted cross-sectional studies, where children of the same age are studied to see what uniformities exist in their characteristics and behaviour; and longitudinal studies which register chronological changes in intellectual and moral development. Large numbers of children have been measured and tested under controlled conditions. The result has been a body of detailed and disciplined information, so that we now know more accurately than ever before what children are like at different ages and under different environmental conditions. Alongside this detailed empirical enquiry has gone on the work of Freud and his followers, no less illuminating in its way although more intuitive and less scientifically rigorous in its methods. From this mass of work, which has increased our understanding of children beyond anything contemplated by most of the earlier theorists, we will select only two examples, the contributions made by Piaget and by Freud.

(a) *Piaget* Piaget, it should be noted, does not see himself as a child psychologist but rather as a worker in the field of what he calls 'genetic epistemology', the study of the stages by which individuals acquire cognitive maturity. Since, however, his work is mainly concerned with the cognitive development of children, with the stages in which children think and acquire the conceptual frameworks which enable them to make sense of their world, it will perhaps be a pardonable simplification if we include his work under the general heading of developmental psychology. (4) (27, Ch. 19)

Piaget's researches and findings are detailed and complicated and his work is still being carried on. What follows here is not an attempt to give an extended account but merely to indicate the general nature of his conclusions. If allowances are made for over-simplification, these conclusions might be summarised in this way:

(i) Children's thinking, and particularly that of young children, is pre-adult in the sense that it is often of a different kind from adult thinking and not merely low-grade or inefficient adult thinking. The normal adult has acquired a conceptual framework which enables him to see his world as an orderly system, framed in space and time, and made up of objects which persist and causally affect each other. Moreover he can perform complicated logical feats, like distinguishing things as members of classes, and seeing various relationships between things, things as being larger than, smaller than, or equal in size to, each other, for example. He can also abstract his attention from concrete individual things and think in terms of contingencies and hypotheses, of what might be the case. He can, that is, think formally as well as in concrete terms. All this sounds complicated but it is a normal part of every-day adult thinking. Our world is structured by the way we think. Now, it is very easy for an adult to suppose that, since a child is like him in many respects, he will have a mind similar to his own, and that a child's mind works very much as his own does. Piaget contends that this is not altogether true, especially in the case of young children. The young child's mind works in such a way that, to begin with, many of these adult distinctions are not made, or are made imperfectly. The very young child, for example, does not readily distinguish between himself and the world about him. There is a stage where he does not clearly see the world as con-sisting of separate and persisting things. The adult categories of space, time, number, causality, are not always clearly grasped by him. Piaget's point is that the child is not born with adult thinking patterns and at first cannot think as an adult thinks. This is a skill he has to acquire. The implications of this for teachers are obvious and important. Methods of teaching which may be appropriate for adults or adolescents might be most inappropriate for young children. Moreover a teacher must bear in mind the gap which may well exist between her language and thinking in the classroom and that of her pupils. It is sometimes quite difficult for an adult to realise that what seems obvious to him may not seem so to a child whose conceptual apparatus is still non-adult. We see here, incident-ally, an example of the close connection between our assumptions about children and assumptions about methods, and how revised assumptions about the one will have a bearing on the other.

It may be questioned whether Piaget's conclusions depend entirely on empirical considerations, but he has backed up his general point about children's thinking with considerable empirical evidence, and has, to a large extent, reaffirmed Rousseau's remarkable insight, that a child is not, and should not be thought of as, a miniature adult, but is a being with distinctive ways of thinking of his own.

(ii) A child's cognitive development takes place in stages, roughly correlating with the growth stages of infancy, childhood and adolescence. The infant child almost literally thinks with his limbs, exploring space around him and gradually acquiring concepts like those of space and time and a self distinct from the rest of his surroundings. Later on, in childhood proper, his thinking centres on the concrete things of his experience. He learns to count and classify things but at first only in terms of concrete particulars, not in abstraction. He can, for example, arrange a number of sticks or objects in order in increasing or decreasing size, but finds difficulty in answering correctly questions like : 'If Mary is bigger than Helen and smaller than Jane, who is the smallest?' He is, as Piaget says, at the stage of 'concrete operations', where he thinks most effectively in terms of and with reference to concrete objects. At some time between childhood and adolescence he will reach the point where he can operate in abstract terms, independently of concrete material and examples. He can then think in terms of hypothetical situations, about possible future or contingent situations abstracted from the concrete here and now. Piaget calls this the stage of 'formal operations' and this is a characteristic of adult thinking. The main point is that Piaget provides us with an empirically supported version of Plato's insight that the cognitive development of children is normally a progression, through fairly well-defined and predictable stages. This progression may be slowed or halted, and it is possible for individuals to be at different stages in respect of different aspects of their experience. It is not unusual for an adult, normally accustomed to thinking in terms of formal operations, to revert to an earlier stage on occasion. A British Prime Minister once confessed that he could best understand talk about imports and exports when he could work it out with the aid of a box of matches! Children, certainly, may be expected to retrogress in this way in the face of difficult intellectual situations. Here again there are important implications for teachers. What a child learns will be determined to a large extent by the type of thinking he is capable of. If he can only work at the concrete operations level, material and methods which demand formal thinking will be largely wasted on him.

Piaget has also conducted investigations into the development of the child's moral awareness and shown that this too proceeds in stages roughly analogous to his cognitive development. The important point for our purpose here, however, is that Piaget and his followers have produced a considerable bulk of evidence to show what children are like. In so far as this evidence has been arrived at scientifically it provides a reliable basis for those assumptions about children which are required for an adequate general theory of education.

(b) *Freud* Piaget's work has involved some detailed observation of children and their thinking, and the results, whilst not accepted entirely and without qualification by everyone, have a claim to consideration which comes from empirical research. Freud's contribution to our understanding of children presents us with a problem, since whilst his work is not entirely lacking in scientific rigour it rests more upon an imaginative and intuitive approach than does Piaget's. Freud's work is thus more open to the charge that it involves conclusions of an untestable kind, and in so far as this charge is well-founded it shows a weakness in his position. It can, however, be claimed that his conclusions do have empirical support, and that he certainly does give valuable insights into some aspects of human behaviour. The inclusion of an account of his work here has, then, some justification provided that caution is observed.

Freud had little to say which is directly concerned with educational issues, and he was not solely or even mainly occupied with the study of children, as Piaget is. Freud does, however, emphasise the considerable, perhaps decisive, influence of the child's early experiences, especially his early familial experiences, on the development of his personality, and this has an important indirect influence on his educational progress. Freud's work, dealing largely with personality development, is complementary to Piaget's study of the cognitive aspects of development; together they present a picture of the child the teacher meets with in school.

Freud's account of the development of human personality is complicated, and no more than a brief sketch is given here. (27, Ch. 15) The account is given in various metaphorical ways, but essentially, normal personality development is understood as a process whereby a mature and rational being is evolved from a primitive mass of instinctual energy which Freud calls the Id. The Id is a blind, instinctive force which aims at immediate gratification of its desires. It acts according to the 'pleasure principle'. In time, as a consequence of the Id's contact with the world there emerges a more prudent calculating aspect, which Freud calls the Ego. The Ego tries to control the strivings of the Id, adjusting behaviour to conform to the requirements imposed by the external world, and aiming at the overall increase in satisfaction which comes from adherence to the 'reality principle'. The Ego makes use of a number of psychic mechanisms, such as repression and sublimation, to contain and control the primitive energy of the Id which, if left unchecked, would bring distress or disaster to the personality. The account is complicated by a third persona, called the Super-Ego, which is, roughly, a response to the demands made upon the individual by others, by his parents for example, who praise or blame him for his conduct. The Super-Ego operates mainly through the conscience, which Freud regards as the internalised voice of authority, parents or other authority figures. Id, Ego and Super-Ego are thus quasi-personalised categories which represent the basic components of human personality. The development of an individual personality is described in terms of the gradual controlling of instinctive behaviour by the Ego, the more rational aspect of the self. For Freud the fully developed, rational, autonomous person is one freed from the domination of both the Id and the Super-Ego. The Id is totally non-rational, mere instinct. The Super-Ego represents direction from without, authority imposed upon one by others. The mature personality is Ego-directed, rationally determined from within, an autonomous being. Normal development involves conflict between the demands of the Id and those of the other aspects of the self, and Freud sees the mechanism of 'repression' as a means by which the dangerous urges and desires of the Id may be tamed. These urges are 'repressed', hidden away in an 'unconscious' mind, out of psychic sight, as it were. These repressed elements, urges and desires of the 'forbidden' sort, frequently sexual in character, disappear from the conscious mind and are forgotten. They are, however, repressed and not destroyed, and they may continue to operate in subterranean ways, influencing behaviour 'unconsciously'. Freud has some interesting and illuminating things to say about the effects of repressed psychic material, as revealed in dreams, slips of the tongue, tricks of the memory and other seemingly innocent and unremarkable behaviour.

In Freudian terms the ideal pattern of development is from Id-behaviour to Ego-behaviour. The baby is, to begin with, unmitigated Id, but as a result of his interaction with the world about him, and especially his interaction in the family group, he comes gradually under the sway of the Ego and Super-Ego. In this process socially undesirable urges are repressed, especially those sexual urges which Freud thinks are an important part of the young child's life. Freud attributes to the child a complicated sexual development which occurs in stages and which is linked closely with the Id–Ego–Super-Ego pattern. The sex drives come originally from the Id, and are associated with the 'pleasure principle', and

73

only gradually become subservient to the 'reality principle' under pressure from the Ego and Super-Ego. The young child's sex drives are directed towards obtaining pleasure, first from the erotogenic zones of his own body, the mouth, the anus, the genitals, and then, directed outwards, towards others, usually the parent of the opposite sex. This gives rise to the so-called Oedipus complex, in which the boy sees himself as a rival to his father for the sexual possession of his mother. It is at this point that the Super-Ego, the internalised paternal authority, emerges, and the child's sex drives are repressed, to lie more or less dormant throughout the rest of childhood, to reappear during puberty and adolescence.

Where development is normal the Ego gradually gains ascendancy over the infantile Id, and, ideally, over the Super-Ego too. Freudians suggest, however, that many people do not free themselves completely from the influence of the Super-Ego, and so remain 'other-directed', and so not fully developed as persons, throughout their lives.

This account has a bearing on education. Freud's point is that the child must be recognised as a far more complicated being than he seems on the surface. The charming prattler of the infant school is on Freud's view a being driven by deep-seated instinctual urges, sexuality amongst them, and upon whom the mechanism of repression is always at work. This repression and its consequences, although a normal part of development, may sometimes result in disturbed behaviour, tantrums, aggression, and the like, which may affect the child's willingness and ability to co-operate with others and to learn. Freud will not have the child to be 'naturally' good or bad, but as a complex creature whose behaviour is often the result of 'unconscious' forces, the nature of which it is important that those who have to deal with him should understand. Freud thus offers a theory of psychic development which may help us to understand children better and to have more insight into their often perplexing and seemingly unaccountable behaviour. It has already been said that Freudian theory does not stand on the same methodological level as does Piaget's. Freud's work is not straightforwardly empirical in character; it owes much to an imaginative and intuitive approach to the nature of personality. It is also, to some extent, prescriptive, not merely tracing the development from Id-centred to Ego-directed behaviour, but recommending this as desirable. 'Where Id was, let Ego be!' is Freud's message to mankind. To this extent his findings are less than fully scientific in character. It may be said, none the less, that whatever Freud owes to imagination and intuition, a considerable part of his theory rests on his clinical studies into mental disorders of one kind and another, and to the extent that subsequent experimental work by Freudian psychoanalysts gives backing to his account, what he has to say is scientifically respectable. (see also 44)

iii Learning theory

One other aspect of psychological research with important bearings on educational theory is that which deals with the processes of learning. During the past fifty years psychologists have systematised and refined their knowledge of the way in which learning takes place, in animals and in human beings. This knowledge forms the basis of another component of educational theory, the peda-gogical methods which may be assumed as effective in practice and recommended as such.

In the past there have been established two main positions in learning theory, positions which, despite the immense amount of experimental work done of recent years in this field, are still recognisable beneath the more sophisticated versions now in vogue. The first was mentioned in Chapter 3 in connection with James Mill, and may be called 'Associationism'. The other comprises what are called 'Field' theories of learning. Both involve theories of an empirical kind, which attempt to explain what happens when some-one learns something, a fact or a skill. In both cases the account given points to, although it may not explicitly prescribe, certain procedures to be adopted to bring about effective learning. In this section these two positions will be set out briefly, and some reference made to the way they appear in contemporary formu-lations.

(a) *Associationism* Associationist theories tend to see learning as a matter of connecting up separate elements in our experience, to form 'associations'. Central to each version of the theory is the notion of a learner who responds to the impact of stimuli coming to him from without. Such responses may be natural as, for example, when a loud unexpected noise causes us to start involun-tarily, or where a movement close to our face makes us blink. A great number of them, however, are artificial in that the connection between the stimulus and the response is brought about deliberately. The response of 'nine' to the spoken stimulus: 'What are three threes?' would be an example of this. This artificial connection can be made by bringing stimulus and response together repeatedly, by 'associating' the different elements to form a 'stimulus-response bond'. Learning is then seen as a matter of establishing such bonds. The child who is got to respond 'nine' more or less consistently to questions of the 'what is three times three?' kind may be said to have learned that three threes are nine. With some ingenuity all knowledge can be represented as involving correct responses to stimuli. The pedagogical problem is that of getting the correct response to follow the stimulus. Associationist theories assert, generally, that the desired responses will tend to be repeated if, when they do occur, the learner is rewarded in some way and if incorrect responses are discouraged by some form of 'punishment'. The teacher makes known the right response to begin with and rewards it whenever it is made in appropriate circumstances. If the pupil makes the wrong response he is not rewarded. This, in all essentials, was the root idea of the pedagogy adopted, for example, by James Mill.

This theory has been considerably refined by modern association-ists like Skinner and Hull. (27, Ch. 13) Skinner has carried out a great deal of detailed research on the behaviour responses of organisms, noting what happens when the rate and degree of reward and punishment, or as Skinner would put it, the degree of reinforcement, are varied. Skinner's version of this continued structuring of behaviour is usually called 'operant conditioning', the point being that the responses in question are not tied closely to specific stimuli but are rewarded whenever they occur, so that the response will tend to be repeated. This principle of the reinforce-ment of desired behaviour underlies the use of what is called 'programmed learning' or 'teaching machines', which are, basically, devices for the orderly presentation of stimuli and the systematic rewarding of desired responses. Hull has elaborated a theory in this tradition, suggesting that stimulus-response bonds are formed according both to the frequency with which stimulus and response are joined and the degree to which certain responses serve to satisfy some need in the learner. A child, for example, will tend to repeat those responses which satisfy his need for recognition by adults, or his need for praise, so that he will make those responses which tend to evoke notice and praise from his teacher, and so strengthen these particular stimulus-response bonds. Responses which do not have this need-reducing effect will tend not to be repeated. This underlies a common element in all versions of the associationist approach, namely that behaviour closely connected with feelings of satisfaction tends to be repeated, and so learned. The pedagogy implied by such theories involves the selection, by the teacher, of stimuli and responses and the contriving of programmes designed to strengthen the bonds between them, or to reinforce desired be-haviour. This will usually involve repetition, reward, and possibly, though not necessarily, punishment.

(b) *Gestalt theory* 'Field' theories of learning are perhaps best illustrated by the work of the 'Gestalt' psychologists, like Koffka and Wertheimer. (40, Ch. 3) (41) 'Gestalt' means, roughly, 'pattern', and the Gestalt psychologists claimed that when we have a new experience we do not try to make sense of it by linking up the various elements which constitute it by association. Rather, we try to see it as a whole, a pattern, from the outset. We try, that is, to impose some sort of order or configuration on our raw experience. It is difficult to give a brief, convincing example of what is meant, but we might try with the case, quoted above, of the child who learns that three threes are nine. A Gestaltist objection to the stimulus-response account is that the child's merely being able to say 'nine' in response to the stimulus does not constitute his learning in any true sense. The response would be merely verbal. To *learn* that three threes are nine would involve grasping a total situation in which 'three times three' and 'nine' are apprehended as equivalents. To have this grasp is to have what the Gestaltists call an 'insight', and their case is that learning is essentially a matter of having insights into meaningful 'wholes'. We have such insights when we 'see' the point of an argument, or the solution of a problem, or when we suddenly acquire the knack of a skill we have been practising. We grasp the matter as a totality. So, learning, it is maintained, is not a process of building up sequences of ideas, by association, so much as making imaginative leaps to a grasp of a total situation. By implication, the pedagogical methods likely to be most effective are those best calculated to bring about such insights. In practice these would involve not so much an emphasis on repetitive drilling and memorising as on getting pupils to discern patterns of significance in their work. A simple example of this might be the practice of teaching children to read by using whole sentences as units instead of building up sentences word by word.

This is not the place to discuss the merits of these two approaches to the nature of learning and their implications for teaching. It may be suggested, however, that it would be wrong to think of them as necessarily rival or exclusive theories. An alternative approach would be to think of them as both offering ways of regarding aspects of the learning process—a process which may sometimes be understood best as a matter of building up associations of ideas, and sometimes as having insights into the nature of the material to be learned. Some accommodation between the two approaches has already been attempted, and a contemporary view of learning is that it may involve different levels of activity, ranging from simple responses of the associative kind at the lowest levels of comprehension, to more complicated problem-solving moves at higher levels, requiring the kind of grasp and understanding the Gestalt psychologists call 'insights'. (16) Human learning is a very complicated matter, and it is unlikely that any one theory will be adequate to account for all its complexities.

The psychologist's contribution to an on-going educational theory, then, is an extension of our knowledge of children and a refinement of our understanding of the way in which individuals learn. In these respects we are no longer dependent on the crude and sometimes erroneous assumptions of earlier theorists. The findings in this field are by no means free from controversy, but the psychological basis of learning is none the less more firmly established than ever before and the psychological assumptions which underpin educational theorising are, consequently, more adequate for their purpose.

iv *Sociology*

Sociology is a relatively new science and most of the important work done in the sociology of education has been done fairly recently. Educational theorists in the past were, of course, aware of the connection between education and other social institutions, but none of the writers we have dealt with, with the exception of Dewey, could be said to have had any considerable scientific understanding of sociological issues. This was because systematic knowledge of the sociological kind bearing upon education was not available to them. The social insights of Plato and Rousseau and Mill were often remarkably perceptive, but they owed more to intuition and imagination than to rigorous enquiry. No educationalist need be in that position today. A great deal of empirical work on the relationships between society and education has been carried out, and the results go far to provide us with reliable assumptions on which to base educational conclusions.

In Chapter I a distinction was made between theories *about* education and theories *of* education. It was suggested that the sociologist as well as the psychologist could offer theories of either kind. Sociological theories *about* education would take education as a social fact and try, for example, to give some explanations of its purposes and functions, or to show how the impact of other social institutions, like the family and social class, affects educational issues. Sociological theories *of* education would be more like the general theories we have dealt with already, giving some sort of prescriptive message, from a sociological point of view.

(a) *Durkheim* One theory, which combines both approaches, was given by the French sociologist Durkheim (1859-1917). Durkheim was concerned, partly at least, with the function of education as a means to social cohesion. He regarded society as a collection of individuals whose wills had to be brought into some sort of order and uniformity if social life was to go on. Without this discipline society was in danger of disintegrating. This social solidarity, which was exemplified by such things as people keeping the law, fulfilling obligations and maintaining institutions like property and marriage, could, Durkheim thought, be brought about in various ways. One way was to maintain a pattern of rituals, traditions and observances, with an emphasis on loyalty, to authority, to one's kin, to one's locality and to one's religion. This would result in a solidarity or cohesion of what Durkheim called a 'mechanical' kind, brought about by psychological pressures on people to conform to established ways. A primitive tribal society with its uncritical observance of custom and tradition and its ready acceptance of punishment as a way of maintaining its traditions would be an example of a group held together by mechanical pressures. The social solidarity achieved in this way is stable and strong, but more or less unreflective and non-rational in character.

Social solidarity of a different kind, which Durkheim calls 'organic', comes about from the discipline imposed on people who collaborate in some common task but perform different though complementary roles. Here a sense of solidarity emerges from a mutual recognition of the need for co-operation and support. Whereas mechanical solidarity comes from the fact that men are fundamentally similar—members of the tribe, dwellers in such-and-such a place, worshippers at a common shrine—organic solidarity arises from the recognition of significant *differences* between men. The cohesion of the players in a string quartet, or a team of surgeons and others working in an operating theatre, would be solidarity of the organic kind, whereas that of a squad of soldiers drilling on the parade-ground would be 'mechanical', brought about by external pressures of a ritualistic nature. Organic solidarity is thus more typical of advanced societies, where division of labour is more pronounced. (12) Durkheim suggests that no society can exist adequately on the basis of organic solidarity alone. There must be an underlying mechanical solidarity before organic solidarity can occur. For Durkheim education was an important means to securing mechanical solidarity. This, he thought, could be brought about by emphasising the ritualistic and symbolic aspects of education, by emphasis on the authority of the teacher, by appeals to loyalty to the institution, by the traditional forms of regularity and order, and by the deliberate and institutionalised teaching of established social and moral values. So far as the individual was concerned education was the means of 'socialising' him; by initiating him into the social heritage, education both constrained him and at the same time made him a human being. (13) But this socialisation also had the purpose and effect of creating a firm basis for the continuation of society as a living entity. Durkheim did not deny the possibility of securing organic solidarity too, through co-operative and collective work in education. Indeed he thought that as society became more differentiated education would need to become more diverse and specialised and so give opportunities for such co-operation between individuals in social life. But his sympathies tended to lie with the authoritarian, traditional type of education, through which pupils could be moulded into conformity of a mainly 'mechanical' kind.

Two points may be noted about Durkheim's theory. First it is a theory *about* education in that it offers an account, in general terms, of the social function of education as a means of socialisation. But, second, it is also a general theory *of* education, a general theory offered from a sociological standpoint. In fact, it wavers between giving a description of what education does, and giving a prescription about what education *ought* to be doing. In so far as Durkheim is recommending a certain kind of education as likely to bring about the cohesion required to sustain society, he is giving, not a scientific sociological theory to provide us with assumptions from which to work, but a prescriptive educational theory of his own. In this case the assumptions on which his prescriptive theory is based would require scientific and other grounds to justify them.

(b) *Recent sociology of education* In contrast to the ambiguous overall type of theory offered by Durkheim, contemporary sociologists of education tend to restrict themselves to more limited theories, based on detailed empirical researches. These are straightforwardly theories *about* education. They have given, for example, considerable attention to the various social factors which bear upon a child's chances and performances in school, the influences of family, neighbourhood and social class. They point out that the size of the family the child belongs to and his position in it will have a bearing on the amount of attention he is likely to get from his parents and the amount of intellectual stimulus they will be likely to give him. (18—Nisbet) So, too, different types of neighbourhoods will provide differences in cultural background, and these will affect the educational chances of children living in those neighbourhoods. Linked with this, and perhaps crucial from the sociological point of view, is the educational influence of social class. Halsey and Floud and others have drawn attention to the fact that a child's educational chances depend to a large extent on the social class he is born into. (15) (18) Children of working-class parents tend to get less intellectual stimulus and cultural encouragement at home than do children of middle-class parents. Working-class children tend to do less well at school, leave school sooner, and their chances of higher education are less. Here we have sociological generalisations about children of the greatest importance to anyone engaged in educational theorising. This is what the children in most of our schools really are like. Closely connected with these conclusions are those of Bernstein.

(5) Bernstein is interested in the linguistic presuppositions of effective communication and has pointed out that the working-class child speaks and understands a language which is not in all respects the language he hears from his teachers in school or finds in his text-books. The working class, Bernstein says, tends to confine itself to a 'restricted code' in communicating, a linguistically limited way of expressing itself, with simple, stereotyped constructions, much repetition and a limited use of qualifying words like adjectives and adverbs. The middle class will understand the restricted code but it more usually expresses itself in an 'elaborated code', linguistically more sophisticated. Schools are still mainly 'middle-class' institutions so far as their outlook and methods are concerned and generally use the distinctively middle-class mode of communication, the 'elaborated code'. They deal largely, however, with children whose experience and cultural backgrounds are not middle-class at all. This may mean that the working-class child will tend to be culturally disadvantaged at school compared with his middle-class fellows. He may find that the language and the level of abstraction used in school differs from that which he has been used to at home. The child from the middle-class home, by contrast, will enter more easily into the systematic use of the 'elaborated code', since it is already a part of his normal background. Findings of this kind are damaging to the crude overall assumptions about children we met with earlier. Assumptions to the effect that children are fundamentally similar, in being naturally good, or clean slates for experience to write on, or are like plants which unfold according to some innate pattern, seem naïve and unhelpful when compared with what the sociologist and the psychologist can tell us about actual children in school. Plainly, an adequate theory of education must be based on what children are really like and must take account, not only of intellectual and developmental similarities and differences between one child and another, but also of those similarities and differences which arise from the social and economic determinants of the child's life. (see also 23)

Other sociological research has been concerned with the effects of different educational institutions on what may be expected of children of different social backgrounds. The effects of different types of secondary schools, different methods of class organisation, different forms of teacher-pupil relationships, different forms of pupil assessment, have been subjected to scrutiny. An echo of the Durkheim approach appears in the concern given to the effects of schools organised as 'open' institutions, minimising distinctions of subject matter and authority and emphasising co-operation and cohesion of the organic kind, as compared with the effects of schools of the 'closed' type, with an emphasis on traditional structures and methods. A quite recent development in the sociology of education has been an increased interest in the sociology of knowledge, in the function of knowledge as an element of control in society, and the implications this has for educational practice. (46) This work continues and no attempt will be made here to review or assess its conclusions. In these areas the sociologist can provide valuable limited theories about the effects of social arrangements on educational practice. These theories will, so far as they are grounded on empirical research, contribute to educational theory the basis of reliable assumptions about the children to be taught and the institutions and methods which may be used to teach them.

v Conclusion

This chapter might be summarised by saying that an important function of the psychologist and the sociologist of education is that of drawing attention to the limits of what can be done in education. The developmental psychologist says, in effect, 'Children are like this; they develop in such and such ways'. The detailed conclusions are set out in descriptive theories of child development. These conclusions must be taken into account by anyone who wishes to recommend educational practices and programmes. The nature of children sets limits to what can be done with them, and the developmental psychologist points out what these limits are. Likewise, the educational psychologist says: 'Learning will take place most effectively under such and such conditions, since these are most conducive to the formation of associative bonds or to insights into the nature of the material to be learned. If you want children to learn, you must take account of these conditions.' The conditions which determine effective learning set limits to what can be done, and the psychologist draws attention to those limits. So, too, the sociologist says: 'There are certain influences, those of family, social class, language, school organisation and practice, which determine the way children learn in school, the extent to which they learn, and the social consequences of their learning.' These factors depend on the kind of society we have, and change as society changes, but at any given time they, broadly speaking, set limits to what can be done. The educational theorist must take them into account if his recommendations are to be adequate in practice.

In conclusion it is perhaps worthwhile making a point that every student of philosophy learns to live with, namely, that we may not legitimately move from truths about empirical matters alone to conclusions about what ought to be done. The truths of psychology and sociology are not in themselves warrants for our taking one course of action rather than another. To be a guide to practice they must always be linked with some aim, with some valuable end to be realised, and be shown to be contributory to the realising of that end. It is because we want to *educate* our pupils that empirical truths about them and their circumstances are relevant to what we do. Important though the empirical facts are, educational theory depends ultimately on considerations of value.

6

A contemporary model

i *Content and form*

In Chapter 5 it was suggested that whilst new large-scale theories of education are not in evidence nowadays, there is none the less a place for general theory, although any on-going general theory would be more piecemeal and fragmented than the historical theories already discussed. In this chapter we consider what such a theory would involve.

Historical theories of education were products of their time, limited by the knowledge then available and the assumptions about values which prevailed when they were written. This reduces their applicability to present-day situations, and this will be true of the content of any such theory as time goes on. We cannot hope to construct a detailed general theory of education which will hold good in all times and in all circumstances. The specific content of a theory of education must always be regarded as provisional. In this chapter we are not concerned with giving a general theory as such. We shall not be making any particular assumptions about aims or about pupils nor shall we be giving any positive recommendations about what should be done in the classroom. Our task is that of setting out the main considerations which govern the making of any on-going theory of education and to indicate the way in which such a theory might be made.

A starting point will be to distinguish between the content of a theory and its form. The detailed content of a theory, its particular assumptions and recommendations of substance, is liable to change, but what we called its structure is not. The nature of this formal framework has already been dealt with. A practical theory is, formally, an argument which begins with assumptions about ends to be achieved and materials to be worked on and concludes with recommendations that certain things should be done. What we now have to do is look at the structure of one type of practical theory, educational theory, to discover its characteristic and distinguishing features. We have to ask: 'What must be the nature of the assumptions made if the theory is to be an *educational* theory?' Not every assumption which might be made, about ends, about children and about methods, would qualify for inclusion in a theory of education. On the other hand, there are some assumptions which *must be* made if it is to be an *educational* theory. We have to distinguish between assumptions which may be made, and those which must be made. When this analysis has been done we shall have the outlines of a formal general theory. We shall have its structure as a practical theory and an indication of the requirements which a theory of *education* imposes on its specific contents. This will give us the frame, as it were, leaving the detailed contents to be filled in. These detailed contents, including the recommendations for practice, may be derived mainly from contemporary material, from actual commitments to values, and such up-to-date knowledge as is available.

To engage in this analysis we have to make use of discipline which has not yet featured explicitly to any great extent in this book, the philosophy of education.

ii *Philosophy and educational theory*

The role of the philosopher of education, mentioned briefly in Chapter 1, now needs to be explained in more detail. In the past the philosopher was expected to deal with large-scale problems, like the true nature of reality or man's place in the universe, and to give comprehensive accounts of such matters. Many philosophers tried to do this, with varying degrees of failure. In recent years, however, many philosophers have changed their minds about what philosophers should be doing. They are, consequently, less inclined nowadays to offer overall accounts of reality, metaphysical systems, and more inclined to take on the limited task of analysing and clarifying the conceptual apparatus used by other disciplines, and of examining the arguments used in theorising of various kinds. Philosophy tends now to be seen as a 'higher-order' activity, working on the concepts and arguments used at a lower logical level; its concern is with the clarification and justification of what is being maintained at this level. Thus it is appropriate to talk about the 'philosophy of ...' science, or history, or law. This shift of emphasis is revealed in the recent development of the philosophy of education. Formerly, those who, like Plato and Rousseau, offered general theories of education were referred to as 'philosophers of education' and their work 'philosophy of education'. Strictly, however, what they were doing was theorising about education in the sense of giving recommendations for practice, usually backed up by appeals to moral, political, psychological, and sometimes metaphysical and religious considerations. Contemporary philosophers of education, at least those in the English-speaking world, are not usually concerned with offering educational theories of their own, but with the analysis and clarification of the concepts used in educational discourse, concepts like 'education', 'teaching', 'growth', 'experience', 'play' and the like, and with examining the arguments and justifications used by those who do offer theories of education. (21, Ch. 1) When, in Chapter 4, we suggested criticisms of the theories of Plato, Rousseau, Mill and Dewey, we were engaged in some elementary philosophising of this kind.

We can now perhaps see how the philosopher of education can help us in our enquiry. What we want to know is: what are the distinctive aspects of an educational theory, which make it an *educational* theory, and which are independent of any particular content it may have? What are the special requirements imposed on the assumptions written into it? What can be said, in general terms, about the mould into which the specific contents can be poured, to give a contemporary general theory? The answer to these questions can be obtained by an analysis, of a philosophical kind, of the concept of 'education'. Such an analysis has been carried out by R. S. Peters and what follows is heavily indebted to his work in this field. (31, Ch. 1) (21, Ch. 2)

iii *Educational aims*

A general theory of education must, logically, begin with an aim, an assumption of value. Without this the factual assumptions and the recommendations for practice would have no point. In this chapter we are not concerned with any specific aim in education, with producing Guardians to rule the state, or the 'natural man', but with what, in general terms, an aim must be if it is to count as an *educational* aim. So, if we are to postulate an aim for the purpose of analysis it will be merely formal, namely, that the aim of education is the producing of a certain kind of person, an 'educated man'. As it stands this is uninformative, but it need not remain so. We can convert it into an informative proposition by drawing out what is implied by it, by specifying the conditions which would have to be fulfilled before the term 'educated man' would be applicable to any particular person. Since this term will only be applicable to someone who has had, in some sense, an education, this brings us to the point where we need to ascertain what is meant by 'education', or, to use the philosopher's terms, to discover the criteria which govern the use of this term in our language.

The word 'education' may be used in more than one way, ways roughly related to each other, but with certain differences which are important. In one sense 'education' means little more than 'schooling' and is used to refer to the whole paraphernalia of schools, classes, lessons, teaching, examinations—to what might be called 'the system'. In this sense someone could say that he had been 'educated' at such and such a school, meaning simply that he had been to that school, or that he intended to take up a career in 'education', meaning that he intended to become a teacher or an administrator in the system. This is the descriptive use of the term. But there is another sense of the word, where it is suggested that what happens to the individual in school comes up to certain standards, that he is improved by his schooling, that he has acquired certain skills and knowledge and attitudes generally regarded as worth having, that he has some grasp and understanding of what he has learned, and that his life is to some extent enhanced in consequence. This sense of 'education' is normative, or value-loaded, and applies only to what happens in schools and elsewhere which satisfies this criterion of value. These two senses of education are connected, obviously, but they are connected quite loosely. The descriptive criteria may be satisfied in circumstances where the normative criterion is not. It would not be self-contradictory, or even unusual, for someone to say that although he was educated at a certain school he could not claim to be really educated. The implication would be that although he received an education in the descriptive sense, that he went to the school in question, what happened to him there did not come up to the standards which would warrant the normative use of the term. The school may have been a bad one, or he may have been a bad or unfortunate pupil.

The apparently truistic aim of an 'educated man' may now be seen to have more point. Since it is an end to be achieved, the implication is that it is worth achieving. *What* is worth achieving is an individual who has been educated in the normative sense. The mere passing through the educational system is not likely to be regarded as a worthwhile end; the only rational reason for wanting anyone to do this is that he should be improved or benefited in some way. This is the assumption of value that constitutes the starting point of any general theory of education, which will normally be concerned with education in this second, normative sense, and aim at achieving some valuable end. The end product is to be someone who has been improved by what has happened to him. This is a formal assumption, deriving from the normative meaning of the term 'education'. It can be argued that this assumption involves others, also of a formal kind, that, for example, the individual should have been initiated into knowledge and skills regarded as worthwhile, and that he should regard this knowledge as having value for its own sake and not simply as a means to some extrinsic end like earning a living. These assumptions linking education formally to the acquisition of knowledge and skill would themselves need justifying, and this would involve us in arguments of considerable philosophical subtlety. (33) It is not proposed to pursue this topic here but merely to point out that supposing, as most people would want to do, that education does imply the acquisition of knowledge and skill, nothing specific as to what will count as worthwhile knowledge is written in here. This would constitute part of the particular content of the theory, and would vary according to different social circumstances. None the less, in any society in which a normative concept of an educated man is held, *some* knowledge, *some* skills, *some* social attitudes must be regarded as valuable and their possession as marking off the educated man from one who is not. In our present society we would most probably require an educated man to have been grounded in mathematics and science, history and geography, literature and, perhaps, art. We would also want to include some other general requirements, closely though not conceptually connected with education, like his being able to play the part of a citizen adequately, to be morally responsible, and to be able to use his leisure creatively. The broad aim of an 'educated man' thus involves a number of separate assumptions of different logical types. There will be formal assumptions concerning improvement and an appreciation of knowledge as such, general substantial assumptions about intellectual development, moral development, aesthetic development, and particular assumptions about what specific areas of knowledge should be entered into. The aim of education turns out to be a highly pluralistic matter.

It is important, however, to recognise that any particular substantial content we give to these assumptions will be liable to change. The knowledge, skills and attitudes we now think valuable may not always be thought so. New forms of knowledge, new skills, different attitudes, may emerge to give a different content to what is regarded as the mark of an educated man. The specific content of education is provisional. What are not provisional are the formal requirements that the person we are trying to produce should have been improved in certain ways and that this improvement should be linked with his initiation into and appreciation of certain kinds of knowledge and skill and social attitudes regarded as valuable.

iv *The nature of children*

The second fundamental requirement of a general theory of education is that it should involve correct assumptions about those being
taught. An objection to some of the historical theories examined
was that the assumptions made about human nature were false,
or if not false then 'metaphysical' in character and not open to
check by any publicly agreed procedures. Plainly, an adequate
on-going theory requires that assumptions made about children
should be as accurate as possible and, moreover, be open to testing
in some way.

The philosopher of education can point out that there are some
assumptions about children which have to be made, in the sense
that they are presuppositions of education having any point at all.
We must assume that children are similar in the sense that they
are to some extent plastic. Education in its normative sense involves
bringing about changes of a desirable kind in individuals, so we
must be able to assume that teaching will have some effect on
pupils, that what they will do in future will be influenced by what
they are taught. There is a close connection between being educated
and learning something, and unless children were to some degree
malleable there could be no sense in which they could be said
to learn anything. Learning involves the modification of behaviour
by experience. Again we must assume that children are free to
enter deliberately into the various programmes devised for their
improvement. The concept of education involves not only the
acquisition of worthwhile knowledge and skill but also the implication that the pupil takes part, knowingly and deliberately, in the
enterprise of improving him. Participation by the pupil is a criterion
for the application of 'education' in its normative use, and participation is possible only to a free agent.

That children are plastic and free to participate in what is going
on are formal assumptions, in that they are presuppositions of the
meaningfulness of 'education' in its normative use. They may be
verified by an appeal to what we understand by the term
'education'. But some general, substantial assumptions about
children are also necessary in the sense that, unless they can be
made, education as a *practical* enterprise could not go on. One
such assumption is that children not only change as a result of
what happens to them, but that they change and develop in certain
orderly and predictable ways. Unless we could make this assumption we simply would not know how to go about the business of
educating them. Another such assumption is that the child's grasp
of cognitive and other issues is a function of his socio-linguistic
development and that knowledge and skill can be thus com-

municated to him. These assumptions are general in that they are about a basic similarity in all children, but they differ from the assumptions about plasticity and freedom to participate in that they are not conceptually connected with the concept of education. Unless we could assume that children were plastic and free the very concept of education would be meaningless. The general assumptions that they develop in specific, well-defined, predictable ways, or according to specific linguistic experiences, rest on matters of fact and may be checked by observation and experiment. Such assumptions are essential to any education, in fact, taking place, but the normative concept of education does not depend on their truth for its meaning.

Granted these various assumptions, questions about the actual mechanisms of child development, about the precise nature of various developmental patterns and about how and when they occur, as well as the actual manner and degree of the influence exercised by social and linguistic factors, will be fairly open questions. So too will questions about *how* and to what extent children can be altered in respect of their behaviour, and what effects different regimes of teaching and training will have on them. This is why researches into child development, longitudinal and cross-section studies, follow-up enquiries, sociological investigations into the influence of family relationships, peer-group relationships and the like, need to be carried on concurrently with educational practice, so that teachers can be kept up-to-date with what is known about the children they teach. The important point, however, is that we cannot have particular substantial assumptions about children prior to experience of them, or independently of such experience, or which will be reliable and stand for all time. Educational theory certainly rests on some prior assumptions about children, that they can be changed and that they are free to enter into activities arranged for them, but this is as far as we can go without reference to empirical enquiry. Any substantial assumptions must derive their specific content from the findings of those working in the field of child study. These findings amount to scientific hypotheses about children and are likely to change as new knowledge becomes available. Any assumptions based upon them are themselves only provisional.

v *Knowledge and methods*

Assumptions about the nature of children are either formal or, in so far as they are assumptions of substance, involve matters of empirical fact. Assumptions about the nature of knowledge and the methods used to impart it involve in addition considerations of value. For education in its normative sense to take place, something worthwhile must be aimed at, and this is usually understood in terms of knowledge and skill. Two assumptions about the nature of knowledge are essential to a general theory of education, and for convenience of exposition, 'skill' and 'attitudes' will be included here with knowledge. First, it must be assumed that knowledge is possible, and second, that some knowledge is worth having, either intrinsically, or instrumentally, as the basis of a good life. These assumptions are formal and necessary, in the sense of being presuppositions of any education at all. Unless there was some knowledge to be had, and some was worth having, the concept of education as we know it would have no point. A general assumption of the substantial kind would be that such knowledge is capable of being organised and systematised in such a way that it can be taught and learned. Nothing is written in here as to *what* knowledge is worthwhile, merely that some is. Assumptions about particular areas of knowledge to be learned, skills to be acquired, and attitudes to be adopted, would form part of the particular content of the theory, and would need to be justified in terms of the end they are required to serve. Nor is anything assumed about the logical status of knowledge, whether it is fundamentally a single mode of experience or whether it consists of a number of distinct forms of understanding, each with its own conceptual framework and procedures. A decision on this point would, as was pointed out in Chapter 2, have a bearing on what was recommended for practice. If knowledge is, as has been argued by P. H. Hirst, (19) (21, Ch. 4) a system of different areas of understanding such that no one area, mathematics or science or art, for example, could be a substitute for any other, then this would have an important implication for the kind of curriculum to be recommended. Education would involve initiating the pupil into each one of these distinct forms, separately, either as separate subjects or as combinations of subjects. If, on the other hand, knowledge is a unity, a kind of seamless robe, with no logical divisions, then it would be possible and perhaps economical to educate through a concentration on some aspect of the whole which gave the maximum amount of insight into other aspects of the continuum. This would, no doubt, involve a different approach to the curriculum. This issue need not be debated here. A formal general theory of the kind we have in mind would be neutral on this point. A decision about the logical status of knowledge would result in a limited, particular theory of teaching, depending for its validity on the strength of the epistemological arguments used to support it. If it were sound, its place would be amongst the methods recommended by a general theory of education of the substantial, practice-guiding kind.

The philosopher of education may now make the point that not only must something worthwhile be learned if education is to take place, but that certain requirements concerning how this learning is to be brought about must be met. Thus, to say that education is taking place is to rule out the suggestion that methods like torture or hypnosis or, perhaps, indoctrination, are being used. The assumption here is that the methods used are morally acceptable. (32) Another assumption, to recur to a point made earlier, is that the methods are such as to allow the pupil to participate in the enterprise of getting him to learn. It is not just a matter of his being a passive receiver of instruction; to be an initiate he must take an active part in the proceedings, seeing them as relevant and important to him. Without this proviso education in its normative sense is not going on at all. These assumptions, that the methods used are morally acceptable and permit pupil participation, are formal, necessary in the sense of being presuppositions of education. A general assumption of substance would be that the methods used are within the pupil's capacity to understand them and profit by them. We must, obviously, assume that the methods recommended are capable of being adapted to the pupil's age and intelligence, since without this education could not be carried on in practice.

Again, nothing concrete is being said here about what particular methods are to be used. What will count as morally acceptable will vary with time and place. Dr Keate and Dr Arnold thought it morally acceptable to flog their pupils into industry and order. Few teachers would endorse Keate's methods today. We would, no doubt, rule out hypnosis and brainwashing on moral grounds, but it is possible that one day these methods may be accepted as morally justified. So no specific assumption about the desirability or otherwise of any particular pedagogical methods would be appropriate to the outline of a general theory we are discussing here. We do not even have to assume that education should take place in schools—a point made by the contemporary 'de-schoolers'. The only assumption that this kind of general theory must make is that the methods recommended should not be objectionable on moral grounds. Similarly, all that is required by the general theory is that the pupil should be able to participate in the task of improving him. How this participation will be realised in practice, what specific form it will take, will depend upon a number of circumstances, upon the age and abilities of the pupil and the resources of the teacher.

A further assumption about methods is that they will be effective. This assumption may not always be necessary in the formal sense, since education may be thought of as a task rather than as an achievement, (32) and in this case it would make sense to talk of 'ineffective' or 'unsuccessful' education. But if education is to be understood as an achievement, the making of an educated man, this assumption is formally necessary and as such needs to be written in to a general theory, the point of which is to offer prescriptions for successful practice. Beyond this we cannot go without recourse to observation and experiment, since *what* pedagogical methods are as a matter of fact effective will be a matter for discovery and liable to change. Practising teachers, educational psychologists, sociologists and others are able to scrutinise the methods in use in schools, to check their effectiveness, and, where necessary, recommend their modification or replacement. New and improved methods are always likely. So a general theory of education in the formal sense in which we are now using the term cannot, as such, recommend the 'play way' or 'activity methods' or 'learning by discovery' or the 'integrated day' nor any other specific pedagogical techniques. Nor can it take sides in any controversy as to whether school should be organised so as to concentrate on the 'organic' solidarity of the 'open' type, or on the more mechanical pressures of the 'traditional' model. All these may be appropriate and effective given the right circumstances, and it will be the individual circumstances of the school, class, child and teacher which will determine what methods and what organisation may be used most effectively. All that requires to be done here is to point out that the methods recommended must, in addition to being morally acceptable and allowing pupil participation, be pedagogically effective, and the assumption that they are so would be a component in a general theory of education.

One final point needs to be made about the relationship of actual pedagogy to educational theory. Which methods do in fact conform to the criteria of effectiveness will form the conclusions of various limited theories, theories of teaching, motivation, class control and the like. These too will always be provisional and, moreover, fairly general in their scope. This needs to be emphasised since student teachers are often disappointed to find that educational theory, even particular and limited theories of teaching, does not usually tell them how to deal with specific crises—with this recalcitrant class or that naughty child. But to expect it to do this is to ask more of educational theory than it is able to give. All that a limited theory can do is to give broad recommendations about methods and procedures, leaving it to the individual teacher to adapt and apply these recommendations in practice. Teaching is far more of an art than a science. This limitation is even more stringent when we are dealing, as now, with the formal outline of a general theory. This merely sets out the assumption that some methods, rather than others, should be regarded as *educational* methods, and indicates in general terms why this is so.

vi *The content of general theory*

The requirements governing the assumptions made in a general theory of education having been set out, we can now summarise the argument of this book. It is this: The historical general theories of education discussed earlier on had certain shortcomings. Some rested on assumptions only partly true, or dubious. All were limited in that knowledge now available was not available when they were written. All were to a large extent imprisoned by assumptions which depended on the social climate of their time. These theories are now in details outdated, or are in other ways inappropriate as sole guides for practice. Their main practical value now is that they may draw attention to important aspects of education which might otherwise be given less than their due. Moreover, since the writers were men of considerable ability and insight, not to say genius, what they have to say is, despite its limitations, usually illuminating and frequently helpful in practice. None the less we must recognise that their work now needs to be supplemented by insights gained from new accessions of knowledge and different educational perspectives. Now, the fate which has overtaken the historical theories will overtake any such attempt at a substantial general theory. Any such theory, however general it may be in the way of providing a comprehensive view, will turn out to be particular in that it will depend on particular factual and value assumptions, anchored in a certain time and place. It might then be asked: what is the use of such large-scale attempts? Could we not forget about them and be content with merely limited theories of a pedagogical kind, with recommendations about child management and teaching based on current knowledge?

It is suggested here that we could not; that there is a place for a general theory of education, and that limited, pedagogical theories always presuppose a general theory of some kind, whether recognised or not. Any pedagogical recommendation must follow from assumptions about what is to be achieved, about the human material to be affected, and about the actual methods recommended, that is, from a general framework of assumptions such as we have been discussing. What can be avoided is the kind of general theory which involves fixed, once-for-all assumptions of a supposedly substantial kind, about children and methods, and which goes on to make universal prescriptions of substance, as did those of, say, Rousseau or Mill. Such theories will inevitably be overtaken, by new knowledge, changed notions of value, and be left as impressive monuments on the educational road. To avoid this, the kind of general theory suggested here is formal rather than substantial. Its form can be set out very simply : Granted that we are to achieve educated men, then, on the basis of what we currently know about children and their development, we should initiate them into what we can justify as worthwhile knowledge, skill and attitudes, using such methods as satisfy the canons of morality, pupil-participation and effectiveness. This epitomises the formal assumptions discussed in this chapter, but, of course, as a formal prescription it gives little information of a practical kind. Its very formality, however, prevents it from becoming out of date or redundant. What must be done, for practical purposes, is to fill in this formula with such specific assumptions of substance as will meet an on-going educational situation.

Thus, as was suggested in an earlier chapter, the practising teacher may, within this general framework, give content to his own theory of education. This will not give a general theory in the sense of providing a set of prescriptions of universal validity, to be applied at all times and in any context. The result will, however, be general in that it provides an overall approach to the enterprise of education. It will also be particular in that it will depend for its specific content on present day knowledge and assessments, and it will be flexible in that it will be recognised that the specific content is constantly open to challenge and revision. The general theory, like education itself, will be an on-going concern, changing in content as circumstances require.

Let us now see what this would involve. The teacher, in posing the question : 'What should I be doing in my classroom?' is really calling for the kind of guidance that a general theory of education can give. He is confronted, at the outset, with the formality of an educational aim; his task is to produce educated men and women. What specific content he will give to this, what substantial assumption he makes about the nature of an 'educated man' will depend upon his own personal decision. For one teacher it may be the 'Christian gentleman', for another, 'the well-integrated personality', for another, 'the rational man' or the 'democratic citizen', or perhaps the 'dedicated communist'. There is no one correct answer to the question : 'What, in substantial terms, constitutes the educated man?' The only limits placed on decision here are the conceptual requirement that for anyone to be an educated man he must have been improved by an initiation into what is considered to be worthwhile knowledge and have come to care for what he learns for its own sake, and the practical requirement that the aim should be capable of realisation. Within these limits the aim may be variously formulated, and its formulation will require a

A CONTEMPORARY MODEL

judgment of value, which will stand in need of justification. The justification of such judgments lies in the province of ethics and it is here again that the philosopher may be able to help. The philosopher will not, generally, put forward aims in education himself. He will, however, be able to show the ways in which such aims may be appraised, by indicating the various moral arguments which could be called on to support or criticise them. Educational objectives will rest on some moral position, although it may be that ultimately their justification will depend on a deliberate decision as to what is to count as morally relevant. (31, Ch. 3) The important point here, however, is that the overall aim should rest on some deliberate moral commitment, not on some 'metaphysical' or otherwise untestable assumption about man's nature.

To realise in practice the aim of an 'educated man', however this is formulated, account must be taken of those to be educated. If the theory is to be adequate the assumptions made here must be as accurate as possible. One could hardly make correct assumptions about the most effective methods to employ except on the basis of an adequate understanding of what children are like. What is required is not anecdotes about children or metaphysical assumptions about them but well-attested information about their development, their needs, their intellectual, physical and emotional variety. For this we must go to those able to give authoritative guidance, to the child psychologists, the educational psychologists, the sociologists, to Piaget, to Freud, and to other systematic observers of children. The conclusions based on the detailed observations of these specialists are crucial since they indicate limits to what can be done in the education of children. Again, it must be emphasised that any such conclusions are open to challenge and modification. Child study is an on-going, scientific concern. For education to take place at all children must be alterable and capable of participation in what is done with them. The extent to which children meet these requirements and the way they do so is always a matter for empirical enquiry. Recognition of this fact would keep an on-going general theory of education relevant and alive.

Lastly, the teacher must recognise that, within the limits set by the conceptual requirements, what is taught shall be regarded as worth learning and that the methods used to teach it should be morally acceptable, involve pupil-participation and be effective, what is taught and what methods should be used are matters on which the last word is not likely to be said. What will constitute a worthwhile curriculum will depend on moral and social as well as epistemological considerations. Plainly, a good deal will depend on the specific form the aim of education takes. The curriculum appropriate for producing the Christian gentleman will differ from

96

that appropriate for the making of the dedicated communist. Decisions about the curriculum will be influenced by the teacher's own personal commitment to values and by what the philosophers of education have to say about the nature of knowledge and about the justification which can be given for adopting some knowledge and skills in preference to others, why mathematics and science should be included in the curriculum, for example, and not other 'worthwhile' subjects like, say, heraldry or billiards. This is by no means a simple matter and the case for a 'compulsory' curriculum involves some subtle arguments. (42) What pedagogical methods meet the requirements imposed by the concept of education is, again, a matter of judgment, and the teacher will be influenced by moral decisions about the acceptability of methods like, say, rote-learning or machine teaching. To judge the practical effectiveness of such methods, or of forms of organisation like the 'open' school, the 'integrated day' or the 'traditional' classroom, he will need to supplement his own experience by advice from those able to give expert guidance, those who have conducted research into the effects of teaching methods and ways or organising instruction. Here too the point needs to be made that the methods and forms recommended or adopted are always open to challenge and may be improved, developed, or abandoned as further experience suggests.

In this way, by writing in the particular substantial content drawn from various sources, the teacher can make an on-going theory of education which will be as up-to-date as he cares to make it. Its great virtue will be that it is adaptable and progressive in the sense of being constantly open to revision and change. Its claim to be worthy of acceptance will rest on the degree to which its various components are open to rational justification, or, in other words, the extent to which it is capable of withstanding attempts to show it inadequate.

vii Conclusion

Behind all intelligent practice in education there are certain principles, prescriptions directed to teachers and others. These principles, the practical conclusions of educational theory, are general in that they go beyond references to merely local or short-term teaching situations. They are general principles of *education* in that they comply with certain conceptual requirements which follow from our understanding of what education in its norma-tive sense involves. Examples of such principles would be those to the effect that we should teach, say, mathematics, or science, or history, in ways which accord with the developmental stage reached by the pupil, which illumine his understanding of the world he lives in, which engage his interest and secure his active participation, and which conform to our notions of what is morally justifiable. Such principles need to be particularised in practice, to meet the needs of this child or that class. They derive, ultimately, from our educational aims, from what is considered valuable in human experience, and from a growing body of empirical knowledge about children and teaching methods. Their actual translation into practice is always open to scrutiny and modification. In default of successful challenge they remain relevant to what is done in schools.

A teacher who wishes to be securely based in his professional work must have a general theory in this sense. He must be clear about his aims and the extent to which they can be justified. He must have knowledge of the methods most likely to realise those aims, and knowledge of the pupils upon whom the methods are to be used. Taken together these will give him the general prescriptions he requires and which may be applied in the particular circumstances of his classroom. Such a theory will not have the deductive elegance of a logical system. It will not proceed from self-evident axioms to incontrovertible conclusions. At each step there will be room for hesitation, dispute and readjustment. The structure of the theory will be somewhat loosely connected, but for practical purposes it will be close enough and the whole point of an educational theory is that it should serve a practical purpose.

Since the detailed content of such a general theory will be a matter of personal decision on the evidence available, there will inevitably be differences of emphasis in the theories actually adopted. Some teachers will accommodate themselves fairly comfortably under one or other of the 'traditional' or 'progressive' headings. Others may regard these labels as giving different but not incompatible perspectives and look to insights from both. What is important is not that a teacher should entrench himself firmly in this position or that, but that he should recognise the need for the theory he holds to be rationally defensible. It was stressed in the earlier part of this book that a general theory of education was just as much subject to scrutiny and criticism as a scientific theory and that to be acceptable it must lay itself open to at least the possibility of reasoned rejection. This means that the teacher must hold his positions undogmatically. He must be prepared always to give good reasons for his assumptions and to change those assumptions when good reasons for them are lacking. He must be prepared to submit his arguments to rational examination and possible refutation. For only then will the theory he holds have a claim to validity, a claim no less important than one to relevance and practicability.

Further reading

The texts of Plato, Rousseau, Mill and Dewey given in the general bibliography provide almost inexhaustible reading material. A sound, rather solid, commentary on Plato is R. L. Nettleship, *Lectures on The Republic of Plato*, Macmillan, 1961. W. H. Burston, *James Mill on Philosophy and Education*, Athlone Press, 1973, gives a critical but sympathetic review of Mill's philosophy in its relation to his educational theory. The following will be found useful: R. Archambault, ed., *Dewey on Education—Appraisals*, Random House, New York 1966; L. F. Claydon, ed., *Rousseau*, Collier-Macmillan, 1969.

J. Flavell, *The Developmental Theory of Jean Piaget*, Van Nostrand Reinhold, 1963, is detailed but difficult for a beginner. Piaget's own *The Child's Conception of the World*, Routledge & Kegan Paul, 1964, would be a good introduction to his writing. Freud gives a clear exposition of his own ideas in *An Outline of Psycho-analysis*, Hogarth Press, 1949. E. R. Hilgard, *Theories of Learning*, Appleton-Century-Crofts, New York, 1956, gives detailed treatment of the learning theories covered in the book. Robert A. Nisbet, *Émile Durkheim*, Prentice-Hall, New Jersey, 1965, includes a number of essays covering most aspects of Durkheim's work.

R. S. Peters, *Ethics and Education*, Allen & Unwin, 1966, is a seminal book in the philosophy of education. Part II, dealing with the ethical basis of education, is particularly important. R. F. Dearden, P. H. Hirst and R. S. Peters, eds., *Education and the Development of Reason*, Routledge & Kegan Paul, 1972, is a collection of papers covering a wide field in the philosophy of education.

Bibliography

1 ALEXANDER, P., A Preface to the Logic of Science, Sheed & Ward, 1963.
2 BANTOCK, G. H., 'John Dewey' in Education in an Industrial Society, Faber & Faber, 1963.
3 BANTOCK, G. H., 'Émile reconsidered' in Education and Values, Faber & Faber, 1965.
4 BEARD, R. M., An Outline of Piaget's Developmental Psychology, Routledge & Kegan Paul, 1969.
5 BERNSTEIN, B., 'Social class and linguistic development' in A. H. Halsey, J. E. Floud and C. A. Anderson, eds., Education, Economy and Society, Collier-Macmillan, 1961.
6 BURSTON, W. H., James Mill on Education, Cambridge University Press, 1969.
7 COHEN, B., Educational Thought: an Introduction, Collier-Macmillan, 1969.
8 DEARDEN, R. F., The Philosophy of Primary Education, Routledge & Kegan Paul, 1968.
9a DEWEY, J., The Child and the Curriculum, Phoenix Books, University of Chicago Press, 1956.
9b DEWEY, J., The School and Society, Phoenix Books, University of Chicago Press, 1956.
10 DEWEY, J., Democracy and Education, Macmillan, New York, 1963.
11 DEWEY, J., Experience and Education, Collier-Macmillan, 1963.
12 DURKHEIM, É., The Division of Labour, The Free Press, Collier-Macmillan, 1964.
13 DURKHEIM, É., Education and Sociology, Free Press, Chicago, 1956.
14 FLEW, A., An Introduction to Western Philosophy, Thames & Hudson, 1971.
15 FLOUD, J. E., HALSEY, A. H., and MARTIN, F. M., Social Class and Educational Opportunity, Heinemann, 1956.
16 GAGNÉ, R. M., The Conditions of Learning, Holt, Rinehart & Winston, 1964.

17 GRIMSLEY, R., *The Philosophy of Rousseau*, Oxford University Press, 1973.

18 HALSEY, A. H., FLOUD, J. E., and ANDERSON, C. A., eds., *Education, Economy and Society*, Collier-Macmillan, 1961.

19 HIRST, P. H., 'Liberal education and the nature of knowledge' in R. D. Archambault, *Philosophical Analysis and Education*, Routledge & Kegan Paul, 1965.

20 HIRST, P. H., 'Educational theory' in J. Tibble, ed., *The Study of Education*, Routledge & Kegan Paul, 1966.

21 HIRST, P. H., and PETERS, R. S., *The Logic of Education*, Routledge & Kegan Paul, 1970.

22 HIRST, P. H., 'The nature of educational theory'. Reply to D. J. O'Connor in *Proceedings of the Philosophy of Education Society of Great Britain*, vol. 6, 1972, Blackwell.

23 LAWTON, D., *Social Class, Language and Education*, Routledge & Kegan Paul, 1968.

24 MAGEE, B., *Popper*, Fontana, 1973.

25 MILL, JAMES, Essay on 'Education' in *James Mill on Education* by W. H. Burston, Cambridge University Press, 1969.

26 MILL, JOHN STUART, *Autobiography*, Oxford University Press, 1924.

27 MILLER, G. A., *Psychology, the Science of Mental Life*, Penguin, 1966.

28 O'CONNOR, D. J., *An Introduction to the Philosophy of Education*, Routledge & Kegan Paul, 1957.

29 O'CONNOR, D. J., 'The nature of educational theory', *Proceedings of Philosophy of Education Society of Great Britain*, vol. 6, 1972, Blackwell.

30 PERRY, L. R., 'What is an educational situation?' in R. D. Archambault, ed., *Philosophical Analysis and Education*, Routledge & Kegan Paul, 1965.

31 PETERS, R. S., *Ethics and Education*, Allen & Unwin, 1966.

32 PETERS, R. S., 'What is an educational process?' in R. S. Peters, ed., *The Concept of Education*, Routledge & Kegan Paul, 1967.

33 PETERS, R. S., 'Education and the educated man', *Proceedings of the Philosophy of Education Society of Great Britain*, vol. 4, 1970, Blackwell.

34 PLATO, *The Republic*, Penguin.

35 PLATO, *Meno* in *Protagoras and Meno*, Penguin.

36 PLATO, *Phaedo* in *The Last Days of Socrates*, Penguin.

37 POPPER, K. R., *The Open Society and its Enemies*, vol. 1, Routledge & Kegan Paul, 1962.

38 ROUSSEAU, J.-J., *Émile*, Dent.

39 SWIFT, D. F., *The Sociology of Education*, Routledge & Kegan Paul, 1969.

40 THOMSON, R., *The Psychology of Thinking*, Penguin, 1959.

41 WERTHEIMER, M., *Productive Thinking*, Tavistock, 1961.

42 WHITE, J. P., *Towards a Compulsory Curriculum*, Routledge & Kegan Paul, 1973.

BIBLIOGRAPHY

43 WITTGENSTEIN, L., *Philosophical Investigations*, Blackwell, 1958.
44 WOLLHEIM, R., *Freud*, Fontana, 1971.
45 WYNNE, J. P., *Theories of Education*, Harper & Row, 1963.
46 YOUNG, M. (ed.), *Knowledge and Control*, Collier-Macmillan, 1971.